# *Upsize Woman*

# *in a*

# *Downsize World*™

## *Deborah Lynn Darling*

### *Radiance Publishing*

This book is not intended to treat, diagnose, or prescribe. The information contained herein is in no way to be considered a substitute for your own inner guidance, nor for consultation with a duly licensed health care professional.

## Copyright © 1998 Deborah Lynn Darling

Cover photo and illustrations: Sandy Layer
Editing: Pieter Clark Visser

First Edition, 1998
2 4 6 8 10 9 7 5 3 1
Published by:
Radiance Publishing, P.O. Box 98
Garrettsville, Ohio 44231
email address:   darling@apk.net

Printed in the United States of America

ISBN: 0-9667111-2-2
Library of Congress Catalog Card Number: 9892131

*For every woman who has ever experienced self-doubt and a lack of self-love, I dedicate this book to your healing.*

# Table of Contents

# Acknowledgments

I share my love, gratitude and appreciation for everyone who has ever opened their heart to me and helped me grow, for all those who saw my light and potential and helped to guide me to my highest good, and especially for everyone who helped to make this book a reality.

I wish to thank Sandy Layer for using her magnificent artistic talents to create both the cover photo and the beautiful nudes you will see at the beginning of each chapter. Sandy you are a sensational artist with one of the best eyes I have ever encountered. I have had such fun working with you on this project, and have enjoyed getting to know you better. I delight in being able to call you a friend. Incidentally, as well as being a sensational artist, Sandy is also an awesome interior decorator and can be found in Garrettsville, Ohio.

Thanks don't say enough for the gifts that my dear friend Pieter Clark Visser brings to me. Pieter, you are truly a great light in my life. I thank you for your friendship and for your great editing and writing skills. I thank you for staying up until midnight (especially since you are an early morning person) to give me the edits under a grueling deadline. Your talents are great and many, my dear friend, and I appreciate you more than you will ever know.

I want all the world to know that Pieter is a terrific motivational speaker, lecturer, and writer, as well as being a nationally-known voice over and on-camera talent. Pieter's is the male voice you hear on my *Upsize Woman in a Downsize World™* tape series. To reach Pieter call him at (941) 778-8268 or email him at: eaglegroup1@juno.com

I wish to thank Rhonda Jones, owner of Jones Graphic Design, for designing the cover of the book and working under the chaotic deadlines asked of her. Rhonda, I am very happy to have had the opportunity of meeting you and being able to take advantage of your wonderful artistic abilities. You are a magnificent wood carver, as well as a wonderful graphic designer. Rhonda can be reached at Jones Graphic Design in Garretttsville, Ohio. Her email address is: jgd@apk.net

I thank, with all my heart, the Angel Gabriel for helping me to write the book. I was told by Doreen Virtue that when you asked Gabriel for guidance in all forms of communication, he would come through; and come through he did. I am thrilled for his help and delighted to know that I can speak to my angels just by calling them to me. Incidentally, angels like it when you ask for them by name. My experience with Gabriel was so pro-found that I recommend that you all ask your guardian angels for help. Look in the appendix to find out how. Believe me, it works.

From the bottom of my heart I thank my mother, Betsy Heighberger, for believing in me and my work enough to support me on all levels, including paying for the book to be printed. Mom, you have come through for me so many times in so many ways that they are too many to enumerate. I love you and appreciate you more, perhaps, than you will ever know. I thank you for believing in me and my work enough to put yourself on the line, time after time. I want you to know what a radiant light you are in my life. I love you dearly.

# Foreword

The problem with a Foreword is that the reader generally expects to have a pretty good idea about the author of the book by the time he or she has finished the Foreword. Now, usually, that's a reasonable expectation. The general run of authors, after all, while they may be interesting to some degree, are a fairly simple lot, not too difficult to sum up in a couple of pages or so.

But that's the trouble with Debbie. You see, I've known her for the better part of a decade now, and the one thing I've absolutely learned about Debbie is that she has more facets than the Hope Diamond. And, to be sure, she's more attractive, has more sparkle, and in fact is worth a whole bushel of Hope Diamonds.

Her talents are legion, her interests are boundless, and her enthusiasm and vibrancy are, frankly, way beyond my poor abilities to describe them. I've been around words for a long time now, and they seldom fail me, but when I try to explain the wonder that is Debbie Darling, my word well just goes dry.

How can one describe the intensity of her compassion for each and every person she has helped? Or the glow she gets when she talks about—well, about darned near anything that interests her, and believe me, that takes in a whole lot of territory. And as for any attempt to explain what makes this supercharged dynamo of a women tick, I might just as well try to explain the general theory of relativity. I know there's no way I can wrap her up in one little Foreword, so frankly, I'm not even going to try.

One thing I can tell you, however: I'd be very surprised if you ever meet anyone who has more fun, has helped more people, has more friends, loves life more, gets a bigger kick out of any kind of good music, has more talents, enjoys more interests, knows more about making injured people whole again, or has more admirers than Deborah Lynn Darling.

I should mention one other thing, You may not embrace every single approach you find in this extraordinary book (I certainly can't recall the last time I endorsed and accepted everything I found in any book), but I can guarantee you this—you will find a number of things between these pages which will enrich your life, increase your measure of health, and broaden the horizons of your world. And when was the last time you got anywhere near that much value in a book? Not lately, I'd guess.

So get set to learn, enjoy, and grow. Allow me to introduce your two new best friends—the person you're about to become, and Debbie Darling.

Pieter Clark Visser
October, 1998

# *Introduction*

Blueberry Hill is my home. I bought it over ten years ago - repaired, refurbished and redecorated it with all my love. In return it has loved me, nurtured me, protected me from the elements and has kept me safe and warm. It has been my rest, relaxation and salvation - my calm amidst the storm.

I truly loved my new home but was afraid that it, like so many people and things I had loved before it, would be taken away from me. While I have a family, I had seldom felt loved by them. While people seemed to like me, I had always felt as though I was an outcast - the black sheep so to speak. My childhood wounds were deep. I desperately needed and wanted a place to call home. A place where I could be me, without the negative judgment of others.

With my fears in tact, I kept my home and its healing properties to myself—insuring it's safety in my own mind. And then one day, I awoke and realized that I was healed. I felt loved and nurtured and at peace with or without the approval of others. The house I bought so many years ago had loved me and made a home for me. I knew it was now time to open my home and its healing properties to others. I knew that what the house had given to me could never be taken away. And so, I created a program where women could come, without judgment to feel loved, nurtured and cared for, just as I had been.

In my travels and in my capacity as Director of Blueberry Hill Retreat for plus size women, I have had the greatest opportunities of working with women to help them gain greater self esteem and self love. My work in this area has lead me to believe that everyone can achieve self love by changing their focus. When we take our focus off the negatives and place it on the positives, we naturally see more positives in our lives.

The week long program teaches women how to increase their self esteem and gain self love and respect. I never dreamt that this program would be as miraculous for some as it has been. And I especially never dreamt that it would change my life so profoundly. I am a firm believer that we teach best by example and through becoming an example, I have created greater joy and happiness in my own life as well as the lives of my clients.

I thank God every day for this lovely house that has given me a home that I call Blueberry Hill. But mostly I thank God for bringing this house into my life as the catalyst to see my own inner light and beauty. This house and I are one. The peace that one feels here is my inner peace, the beauty is my inner beauty brought forth to share with others.

Ten years ago I bought a house. I didn't have a clue the magnificence it would bring to my life. Perhaps it's more accurate to say that I didn't have a clue that that magnificence was within me all along just waiting to be brought forth. I do now, and I want all of you as well to experience the magic of Blueberry Hill.

I am writing this book so that each and every one of you can experience the real you, the beautiful you, the magical you that is already there waiting to be seen *by you!* I hope that by writing this book you will begin to use some or all of the techniques that we teach here at Blueberry Hill.

I wish to support you in your efforts to become the best *you* possible and hope that during the process you will be patient and kind to yourself. Imagine that I am there with you as a constant reminder of the magnificent person you already are. Your light can never be turned off, it can merely be dimmed or brightened. You're about to brighten your light for all the world to see.

When you believe you're as beautiful as I know you to be, you'll see beautiful. What a gift that day will bring to me. God bless!

Deborah Lynn Darling
October, 1998
Garrettsville, Ohio

# List Your Top 20 Strengths:

1). _____
2). _____
3). _____
4). _____
5). _____
6). _____
7). _____
8). _____
9). _____
10). _____
11). _____
12). _____
13). _____
14). _____
15). _____
16). _____
17). _____
18). _____
19). _____
20). _____

"Any fool can criticize, condemn, and complain. And most fools do."

—Dale Carnegie

# Downsizing

I am an *"upsize woman in a downsize world."* But it hasn't always been a downsize world. The bodies of women just like me have defined beauty throughout the ages. Go into any museum in the world and you'll find us displayed there as the quintessential example of beauty. We have been portrayed by the greatest artists of all times— Rubens, Rembrandt, Titian, Boticelli, to name but a few.

Leonardo DaVinci created what many consider to be the most beautiful (and certainly the most famous) female portrait in existence—the Mona Lisa. You don't have to look too closely to see that Mona would definitely be considered an upsize woman by today's standards.

For centuries my body has been regarded as the epitome of beauty and sexual delight—the absolute ideal. My voluptuous curves have made the strongest men go weak with desire. I have represented the goddess energy, mother earth, creativity, fertility, sensuality, and raw desire. My soft lush body with sweet tantalizing breasts and wide hips

15

has been ripe for making love, fertile for creating children, and infused with true nurturing gifts.

I am the same woman today as I have been throughout time; but today I find myself in a world caught up in a downsizing craze. It has downsized corporations, cars, families, candy bars, etc. Now, it's trying to downsize me—and you.

This downsizing craze, however, is a relatively new phenomenon. As recently as the end of the 1800s Lillian Russell was the sex symbol of the day, weighing in at 226 pounds. Men would have sold their souls to spend one night with her. Women would have given just about anything to look and be just like her, in hopes of creating the same desires in their husbands that Lillian was capable of creating.

"Golden hair united to brown or hazel eyes, soft, smooth skin with faint olive shading, little color in the cheeks, features sharply defined (although relieved by a slight facial fullness) and the figure healthily rounded." These were the attributes of perfect beauty set forth by one Cosmopolitan writer in 1890.

For centuries, a body with some meat on its bones defined prosperity and aristocracy. In America, a fleshy body indicated great

16

wealth and prestige. Foods that were capable of making you fat (or the ability to afford large enough quantities of food to make you fat) definitely evoked an image in one's mind of the well-to-do.

When it became possible for lower income people to become fat, the glamour disappeared. This, together with the new influx of rich, slim European travelers to the United States at the beginning of the 1900s, created the new "thin is in" fad. It seemed that the wealthy Europeans traveling to this country on business were all quite thin and healthy. Spas were the "in" thing in Europe, and since only the rich could afford to go to a spa, wealthy and thin became synonymous.

This gave rise to the 1920s flapper girls, and for the first time, women took on a more androgynous look. The flapper girl gave up her voluptuous curves for a more masculine straight up and down appearance. She left behind her goddess, mother earth energies and adopted a more daring, competitive, even somewhat masculine character.

While this new woman was daring and exciting, she seemed to lack the nurturing qualities exemplified by women of the past. So it wasn't long until the Gibson Girl appeared. The Gibson Girl retained many of the daring elements of the flapper girls, while restoring some of the mother earth qualities of the past. This new combination would soon come to be thought of as the "down home girl" look.

The Gibson girl wasn't *real*, however. She was an illusion, created in a man's mind for advertising purposes; yet she would become the first example of the unrealistic man-made media ideals we women would soon be struggling with on a regular basis.

While women experienced some relatively drastic downsizing from the late 1800s to the 1920s, it wasn't long before voluptuous bodies were back in style. Breasts were back in style. Being feminine was back in style. Sexy was back in style. Jane Russell, Elizabeth Taylor, Marilyn Monroe, Jane Mansfield and others oozed sex appeal with their gorgeous, sumptuous figures.

Marilyn Monroe was a size 16 at the height of her career and was considered by many the sexiest woman alive. That was in the late 1950s and early 1960s; and less than 40 years later Marilyn, by today's standards, would be considered *too fat* for leading roles on the Silver Screen.

Twiggy resurrected the androgynous look, and in doing so gave the fashion industry and the television and print media a shot in the arm. She provided them with the means to create a whole new fashion trend. *No one* looked like Twiggy. But if the media and fashion industries could make us believe that Twiggy was the new definition of beauty, they'd have us flocking to buy clothes and makeup to imitate this new look—*everyone* would have to buy, buy, buy!

We women bought, all right—we bought the whole image, hook, line and sinker. Since the 1960s our eyes have been trained to see an increasingly narrow feminine image—so narrow that Kate Moss and some of the newer models actually make Twiggy look as if she could be plus size.

By today's industry standards a plus size is a size 12 and above, yet *the average dress size in America is 14.* I don't know about you, but I define a plus size as 18 and above. Size 18 and above takes you into a whole new clothing department. I believe a very negative message is being conveyed to women today. Come on, let's be sensible. How can size 12 *possibly* be considered a plus size when 14 is the average?

This craziness simply has to stop. But we can't change the way the industry views us—or the way the world views us—until we change the way we view *ourselves.* When we heal ourselves, we heal the world. My mission is to encourage you to love yourself exactly as you are right *now*—to help you see once again that *you are a masterpiece!*

# What Makes You Happy?

1). _____
2). _____
3). _____
4). _____
5). _____
6). _____
7). _____
8). _____
9). _____
10). _____
11). _____
12). _____
13). _____
14). _____
15). _____
16). _____
17). _____
18). _____
19). _____
20). _____

"Love Yourself First."
—Lucille Ball

# Body Image

How many of us are happy with our bodies just the way they are? Believe it or not, just six percent of the female population are content with their bodies. The other 94% are dissatisfied. Here's a little test: If you answered yes, that you *are* happy with your body, I would then ask you if you'd be willing to get up in front of 1,000 people in a swim suit? If the answer is still yes, congratulations. Your body image has remained intact despite the negative media messages.

If you answered that you liked your body but would *not* be willing to get up in front of 1,000 people in a swim suit, you probably aren't as satisfied with your body as you might think. Don't worry, because together we're going to change that.

Are you currently dieting, have you dieted within the past year, or are you thinking about dieting? Chances are you answered yes to at least one of these. Despite the fact that 98% of diets don't work (and that many are unhealthy to boot), we continue to hang onto the hope that the latest diet fad will be the miracle we've been seeking, the vehicle that will allow us to go to bed looking like ourselves and get up in the morning looking like Raquel Welch. There's no such thing—you can take my word for it.

Have you ever gone to a movie, and after seeing the gorgeous female stars such as Michelle Pfeiffer, Demi Moore, Raquel Welch, etc., played out the following negative self talk scenario in your mind? "I can't believe how gross I am. I am so fat and disgusting. I just can't believe that I have let myself go like this. Raquel Welch has such a phenomenal figure. That's it. I'm going on a diet first thing tomorrow morning. I'll start exercising. As a matter of fact maybe I'll join a health club..."

I'm sure this scenario is painfully familiar. But how about *this* one? You go to the store and buy some CDs by Mariah Carey, Whitney Houston and Barbra Streisand. You listen to these ladies sing and you have this self talk playing out in your mind: "I don't know what I'm going to do. I just can't believe what a bad singer I am. I'm going to call a vocal coach first thing tomorrow morning."

Now, maybe that scenario sounds familiar, but the chances are slim. Yet both examples are exactly the same. You ask how I could possibly equate them? The answer is simple. Both Raquel's body and the three voices are beautiful, and in most cases are not achievable.

You would enjoy the music for its sheer beauty. You wouldn't dream of hiring a vocal coach, because while you might be incorrect in your assessment that you can't sing, you would never dream that you could achieve this level of vocal perfection. Most important, however, is that the media and society are not sending you constant messages that you are unattractive, unworthy and lower than whale slime because you can't sing like Mariah Carey. The fact is that no expectations are being placed on you at all in the singing department. The same world that judges you, criticizes you and ostracizes you for having a fat body couldn't care less whether or not you can sing. That world sees Mariah Carey's voice for what it is—a gift.

That is literally what Michelle Pfeiffer, Demi Moore and Raquel Welch's bodies are—gifts. Those bodies are beautiful, and we can admire them for their beauty, but like the singing voices, they are unattainable for most of us. We don't have *weight* problems—we have *image* problems.

If you don't believe me, just imagine this scenario: You wake up tomorrow morning. You get your first cup of coffee and turn on the television set. You can't believe your eyes when you see little Katie Curic suddenly weighing in around 190 pounds. You quickly turn the channel and there's Joan Lunden, who must tip the scales at 250. You turn to Regis and Kathie Lee—Kathie Lee herself must weigh 280. You hurry and get dressed. You have to get your hands on a newspaper to see what happened between bedtime last night and coffee time this morning.

You get to the newsstand, and there on the cover of Cosmopolitan is Claudia Schiffer, at about 245 pounds; and there's Kate Moss on the cover of Vogue appearing to weigh at least 195. Would you *ever* have to diet again? *Absolutely not!*

The truth is that the simple depiction of some healthy, attractive, plus size role models in the media could totally turn the tide on these negative body images we women are subjected to. A few more Delta's, Rosie's, and Oprah's instead of the stereotypical fat chicks like Mimi on The Drew Carey Show could really make a tremendous image difference for us all.

Let me reiterate: We do not have weight problems; we have image problems. The media provide us with very few role models to aid us in healing our self-image plight, so we have to do it ourselves. We can do this by taking 100% responsibility for ourselves and our lives.

# What Makes You Sad?

1). _____
2). _____
3). _____
4). _____
5). _____
6). _____
7). _____
8). _____
9). _____
10). _____
11). _____
12). _____
13). _____
14). _____
15). _____
16). _____
17). _____
18). _____
19). _____
20). _____

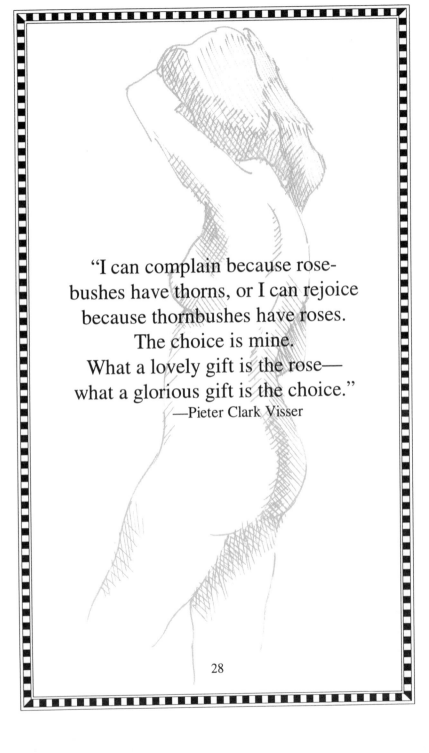

"I can complain because rose-
bushes have thorns, or I can rejoice
because thornbushes have roses.
The choice is mine.
What a lovely gift is the rose—
what a glorious gift is the choice."
—Pieter Clark Visser

# Taking Responsibility

How would it feel to know that you are currently living the life of your dreams? In fact, imagine for a moment that you are 100% responsible for the life you are presently living. Does that sound frightening or impossible to you?

If your life is not at all what you expected it would be, then you probably are shaking your head at this moment and saying that you're not living any life *you* ever dreamt of. You definitely would *never* have chosen the life you're living, or your present circumstances, your body, etc. But the fact is that you have done precisely that.

Whether you believe it or not is irrelevant at this moment. The truth is that taking 100% responsibility for yourself and your life is *very* empowering. It takes you out of the role of victim into the role of CO-creator. As a victim you are always at the mercy of someone else. The only way your life can be better is if someone *else* makes it better for you. You find yourself in a life where placing blame or pointing the finger at others is your primary survival tactic.

Placing blame allows us to shift the responsibility from our own shoulders onto the shoulders of someone else, but it doesn't offer us any solutions for change.

The good news about taking 100% responsibility for yourself is that as a CO-creator you are empowered to *make any changes you please* in your life. If you don't like the life you're living, you can change it at any time.

Sound impossible? Every moment of our lives we're making choices. Some choices are small and seem to have few consequences attached to them, like deciding to brush your teeth in the morning.

If you decide not to brush your teeth one morning, it isn't any big deal. But let's say that one day turns into five, then ten, then a month, etc. When you finally go to the dentist's office for a checkup, you find that you have a mouth full of cavities—a direct result of your choice not to brush your teeth.

It may in fact be possible to go without brushing your teeth for a month and not get any cavities, but the very act of choosing not to brush makes you responsible for the outcome.

Believe it or not, this is good news. It means you can literally start today to create the life that you would *like* to be living, instead of the one that you've settled for. Imagine you can have exactly what you want out of life. You've heard it said that "If you can conceive it and believe it, you can achieve it." Make a promise to yourself right now that you are going to take 100% responsibility for your life and make it a life filled with joy and excitement.

When we really dissect our lives we can see

that they are directly related to the choices we've made. Everything we say and do is a result of a choice we make. Some of these choices are small, like the example of not brushing our teeth. Other choices are larger, and much easier to recognize.

I have a dear friend. We're quite close, and we have a great deal in common; but we made totally different choices in life. She chose to marry and have children. I chose to make my career the focus of my life, so I never married or had children. She raised her family and got divorced and is now entering the working world. In a sense she will have it all—a family, career, etc.

If I had made the choice to get married and have children before pursuing a career, I might have had it all as well. But my decision to make my career first has meant I haven't had children of my own. I regret not having children, but I know that I made the choice and so my regret is all mine. I chose not to marry, and as a consequence I'm still single. On the other hand, I never had to go through a divorce. My friend got married twice and divorced twice. My choice not to marry may have protected me from the pain of divorce. Or it may have kept me from living a life of bliss with my true love. But the fault—or the credit—is mine alone.

Often people try to tell us that we are making poor choices. For example, I dropped out of high school. I truly believed at the time that I had learned as much as I could at that level. Everyone told me I was making a terrible decision, that I would never get into college, or get a good job without a college degree. Nevertheless, I decided to drop out and go to work for a year. At the end of the year I applied to a number of colleges and got into every one I applied to.

Despite what many people said was a bad choice, I made it to college, and now travel all around the world helping women to raise their self esteem. I am living my life's purpose. I made the choices that were right for me, not for my parents, or teachers, or society. For better or worse, *my life is of my own creation.* The choices have been mine; and every day I make new ones, in the continuing creation of my life. Talk about being empowered!

Being happy, healthy, joyful and beautiful are all within your grasp, every day. Creating a better life is as simple as making better choices.

# Changes You Can, and are Willing to Make Now:

1). _____
2). _____
3). _____
4). _____
5). _____
6). _____
7). _____
8). _____
9). _____
10). _____
11). _____
12). _____
13). _____
14). _____
15). _____
16). _____
17). _____
18). _____
19). _____
20). _____

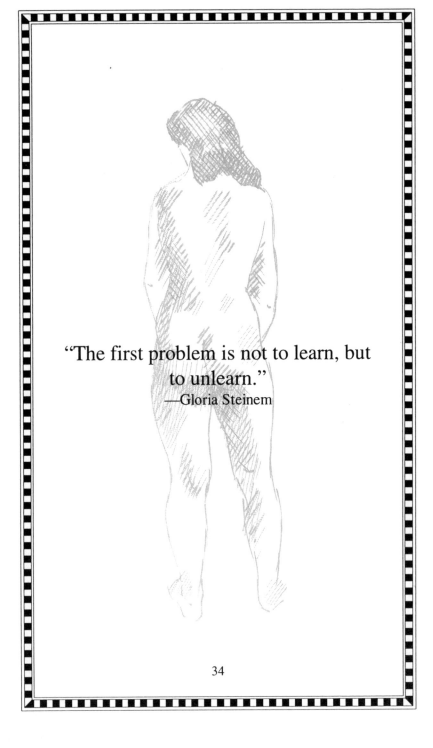

"The first problem is not to learn, but to unlearn."
—Gloria Steinem

# Diets Don't Work

We all know that diets don't work. More and more research indicates that you are better off being overweight than to go on one diet after another— more commonly known as yo-yo dieting. Dieting is 98% ineffective; yet we continue to try one diet after another in our never ending search for a miracle cure for obesity.

The 2% of the dieters who effectively keep the weight off can give credit not to the diet but to the fact that they changed the way they think. They changed the way they felt about food, they dealt with emotional issues without the use of food, they learned not to buy into unrealistic expectations about individual body size, and they learned to love themselves.

Let's do some word associations. I'll give you a word and you respond with the first word or words that come to mind. Let's start with the word "weight". If you're like most people, the first words that come to mind are words like fat, over-weight, ugly, unhealthy, plump, disgusting, heavy, obese, gross, etc.

How about the word "fit"? Did your mind associate this with words like thin, healthy, attractive, exercise, etc.? Most people think of these or similar words when they hear the word "fit". With this in mind, it's easy to see why diets don't work.

At this point I want to tell you three things it is important to know. The first is that what we focus on in life expands. By this I mean that if you focus your attention on anything long enough, you will draw it to you. Have you ever wanted something so badly that you literally couldn't stop thinking about it? If so, you eventually, inevitably, began to think of ways to manifest it in your life.

If you focus on something long enough, with enough concentration and emotion, you will begin to draw it to you. Have you ever had a problem that you thought about constantly? You just couldn't seem to get the problem out of your mind. The more you thought about the problem the more troublesome it became. But as soon as you decided to shift your attention from the problem itself to getting rid of the problem, you found that your mind began to come up with ingenious solutions. When you changed the focus from problem to problem solving, you found the secret to getting what you want.

The second thing it's important to know here is that we live in an abundant Universe. Since the Universe is abundant, it is very hard to lose anything. While it is possible to produce loss or lack in one's life, it is not the natural order of things. It is easier to find than to lose.

Third, the subconscious mind does not hear negatives. Have you ever baked a cake or cookies, found there was one slice (or one cookie) left over?

All day you walked in and out of the kitchen saying to yourself, "I will not eat the cake, I will not eat the cake..." Imagine. You've managed to stay away from the cake all day long. But it's now bedtime and you're making your final pass through the kitchen for the day. Your subconscious knows this is its last opportunity to give you what you've been asking for all day—the cake.

Since the subconscious always wants to fulfill your every desire, it knows that you've been wanting that cake all day. You see, what you thought you were saying and what the subconscious heard were two entirely different things. You said, "I will not eat the cake", and the subconscious, because it doesn't hear the negatives, heard "I will *eat* the cake." That cake literally flies across the room and lands in your mouth, and is gobbled down so fast that you really don't even know how it happened.

What you *do* know is that you now feel negatively about yourself, because you feel you are a failure and a completely useless human being for eating the piece of cake. The fact is, you just didn't know your inner mind's lingo.

*The reasons diets don't work is that the focus is always on the wrong thing.* When we are focusing our attention on weight loss, we know two things right off the bat. First we know that the Universe doesn't readily accept loss, so in order for a diet to produce loss we're going to have to work very hard at it. We know that dieting is not only a difficult process, but it is also emotionally painful, depressing and downright bad for your health. Unhealthy diets range from requiring you to starve yourself, to making you eat far too much protein, to telling you to forget the protein and stuff yourself with carbohydrates. Just about the time I think there cannot possibly be any more silly diets, an even more ridiculous one emerges.

Is a baby that is born weighing two-and-a-half pounds an overweight, fat, disgusting baby? Of course not. The definition of "weight" is "a quantity or a measurement." When I asked you to associate something with the word "fit", I'd be willing to bet that you didn't come up with "a sudden uncontrollable attack", yet that is one of the definitions of the word "fit".

Second, you know that when you focus on weight, you're focusing your attention on the definitions that the subconscious has associated in your mind with "weight", like unhealthy, ugly, overweight, fat, disgusting, etc. When you set a goal to lose weight, or lose a certain number of pounds, you begin the difficult dieting or losing process, in which you literally starve yourself to get those pounds off. The entire time you are focused on a *negative*, on "losing weight". Your subconscious only hears the word "weight, weight, weight." Since it always wants to give you what you want, it waits patiently for the opportunity to do so.

You reach your goal, you abandon your vigilance, and the subconscious steps in and says, "Finally I can give her what she's been asking for—weight, weight, weight." And since the sub-conscious wants to show you how much it really cares about you, and to demonstrate that your wish is its command, it packs the weight on, and usually you will find yourself even heavier than you were before the diet. Why? Because the focus was wrong. Like the old song says, "You gotta accentuate the positive, eliminate the negative..."

"The first wealth is health."
—Ralph Waldo Emerson

# *Fit or Fat*

Baylor Medical School came up with some extraordinary results when they did a study on exercise. They found that you could be up to 100 pounds overweight and be healthier than your thin counterparts who did not exercise. This exciting study revolutionizes the way we plus size women can view ourselves. It literally proves that it can be okay to be fat, but is not okay to be unfit.

If this is truly the case—and we know it is—then why do so many doctors automatically tell plus size people they need to go on a diet, or they'll eventually find themselves victims of such diseases as high blood pressure, diabetes, heart disease and more? Well, the answer is simple. Most plus size people just don't exercise. Doctors are so accustomed to seeing unhealthy, unfit, overweight people who don't exercise, that they have come to believe that fat is synonymous with unhealthy. It just isn't so. Obesity alone is not necessarily a condition that needs to be cured.

How do we become more fit? For one thing, we focus on fitness. We already know that focusing on fitness (or being fit) brings more positives up from the subconscious part of the mind. We know that our subconscious mind is filled with positive pictures that correlate with the words "fit" and "fitness". So instead of focusing our mental attention on negatives, like weight loss or diet, we focus our mental attention where it will do the most good, and create the healthiest, most positive healing environment for us—fitness.

We also know that we can create a healthier, fitter body by increasing movement. We'll discuss more about movement in the next chapter. For now, you just need to know that increased movement is a critical factor in your quest to achieve a healthier, fitter body. As a matter of fact, I believe it is even more important than the foods you eat. And we'll talk about why that's so in the next chapter.

We must change the way we think. We must learn to love ourselves, regardless of our current weight. Without self-love you're beating your head against a wall. What you resist, persists; and if you continue to loathe and hate your fat body, you can never change it. So skip ahead to your 21-day assignment and begin doing the assignment as you're reading the book.

Eat more nutritious foods, especially fresh, living foods. We'll talk about nutrition later in this book, but for now you should start to eat more fruits and vegetables. I'm not telling you anything you don't already know. If it's true that you are what you eat, then you want to be eating foods that will make you strong, healthy and fit.

# Qualities You Like in Others:

1). _____
2). _____
3). _____
4). _____
5). _____
6). _____
7). _____
8). _____
9). _____
10). _____
11). _____
12). _____
13). _____
14). _____
15). _____
16). _____
17). _____
18). _____
19). _____
20). _____

"Think health, eat sparingly, exercise regularly, walk a lot, and think positively about yourself."
—Norman Vincent Peal

# Exercise

It's okay to be fat, but it's *not* okay to be unfit. The key to getting fit is movement. Study after study shows that exercise benefits us in many ways. These benefits include, but are not limited to, raising self esteem, lessening anxiety, helping us to better cope with stressful situations, lifting depression, generally improving mood, improving the immune functions, aiding in better sleep, and energizing us.

All energy is created by the food that we eat and the air that we breathe. When we exercise we not only increase our present energy level, but we also increase our ability to create *more* energy for ourselves—energy we can use in all areas of our lives.

People who don't exercise tend to be more sluggish and have less energy and less enthusiasm for life. Exercise can actually increase your mental ability as well. Exercise helps to provide oxygen to the brain, which helps you maintain mental focus and alertness.

When we starve the body with diets, we literally put the metabolism into survival mode. It slows down because it actually thinks the body is dying. This is why it's so difficult to lose weight. The body has literally shut down the processes that burn the calories. When you increase movement you speed up your metabolism, burning more calories. When you're starting an exercise program it's important to remember that you want to set up a regimen you can keep up with. You also want to choose something that you'll enjoy. If you enjoy the exercise program you've set up for yourself, it's more likely that you'll stick to it. If you think of your exercise as fun and relaxing, rather than hard work and exhausting, you'll enjoy it more.

It doesn't do you any good to start out with a bang, only to fizzle out after a few weeks or even a few days. Set a goal for yourself that is attainable and then stick to it. Statistics show that most people who begin an exercise program have abandoned it after only six months. A lack of enjoyment is probably the number one reason.

Exercise doesn't have to be anything as exhausting as jogging or calisthenics. (In fact, both these activities have been shown to be harmful for many individuals.) Exercise can be as easy as walking. Walking provides great benefits for everyone, and perhaps the thing I like most about it is that just about every person with two working legs can do it.

Walking is an exercise you can do almost anywhere, any time of year. If you live in a climate that gets cold in the winter you can go to an indoor gym or to a mall and walk around. The malls are filled with people who walk for all kinds of health-related reasons. In fact, many malls offer special programs set up just to accommodate walkers.

Check with your local mall.

You hear so much about how important it is to get your heart rate up. That's true, but it is important to *first* focus on movement. As you get more and more fit you can push yourself to move more and more. Don't put the cart before the horse. Becoming more fit is easy. You just gradually increase movement.

Start with 15 minutes a day three to five times a week, and then work yourself up to 1 hour a day, three to five times a week. After you've got the walking part down pat then start to build up speed in your walks. I don't mean to start jogging or running. I just mean push your walk a bit. If you want to add weights to your wrists and ankles when you walk, fine. Nothing too heavy, just little wrist and ankle weights— enough to push you a little bit more in your walk. You'll definitely feel the difference.

Another great exercise is gardening. Gardening, in some instances, works muscles in your body that you haven't felt for years (or at least for a season, for those of you who are avid gardeners). It's a great workout. It's also very good for relieving stress. Studies show that if you work in the garden for as little as half an hour you literally will reduce your stress levels. This is true even for people who don't particularly like to garden.

The earth is extremely "grounding" and therefore connecting with it is a great stress reducer. I used to have a friend who as a child would lie out on the ground and look up at the sky when she was angry. I used to think she was so silly, but she always assured me that it was a wonderful way to get rid of her anger or frustration. Imagine my surprise when, years later, I found that doctors were actually giving her theory some credence.

If you live in an apartment and don't have a garden or access to one, then go out and get some planters and soil and plant some flowers for your apartment. You'll be amazed at how much better you feel. Or go to the park and do some weeding in the flower beds (check first to be sure you won't be arrested). Not only will you be making yourself feel better, but you'll also be helping others to see the beautiful gardens the way they should be seen—with no weeds. This can be a wonderful contribution to your neighborhood.

I also recommend dance, especially ballet, as a terrific form of exercise. Again, take it slow. At Blueberry Hill Retreat we teach yoga. It's non-stressful and low impact, yet the effects on the body are significant. It's great for increasing flexibility, improving circulation, healthier breathing and overall relaxation. It's a total mind-body exercise, and I'm always interested in anything that brings the two together.

More and more movie stars are moving away from calisthenics and aerobics and moving toward yoga. Many people who used to lift weights are turning to yoga. It's kind and gentle to the body, and this is something I particularly like.

I don't believe that exercise means you've got to beat yourself up. Exercise is something you do for yourself because it makes you feel good. When you exercise, your body takes in more oxygen and you're healthier and more energetic. You're able to think more clearly and accomplish more. Perhaps the most amazing benefit of all is that when you start to exercise, your body naturally begins craving healthier foods. That's right! You don't have to change your eating habits if you don't want to. Just start to increase movement and pretty soon, when you've increased movement enough, your body will actually require less food. You'll begin to notice a decrease in your appetite. The food your body does request will be healthier food, which will provide your body with the energy it needs to continue exercising. You'll naturally be drawn to eating more fruits, vegetables and whole grains, and you won't even have to think about it. This change in your appetite and food selections will be a natural process.

When I talk about increasing your movement I don't mean that I want you to get up from the sofa and walk to the refrigerator a few more times a day. I mean I want you to get out in the fresh air and move.

Exercise is one of those things that seems so hard to begin. You can find a million excuses why you don't want to exercise today and why you don't have time, but exercise plays such an important role in our health that if you make excuses not to exercise, I believe you're making the poorest choice imaginable; and poor health is the ultimate outcome.

Exercise is definitely the key to a healthy lifestyle. You'll see the positive effects in all areas of your life—in your body and how your body moves, and in how you feel in your body. You'll see a change for the better in your eating habits. You'll find you have more energy. And one of the greatest benefits of exercise is it's ability to make us feel more positive about life.

Exercise is a great anti-depressant. When we exercise we breath deeply, which creates a higher oxygen level in our system, which in turn releases substances called endorphins into the body, which literally make us feel good. We have a better outlook on life. You've no doubt heard of the "runner's high"? This high doesn't just happen to runners. When we exercise on a regular basis we feel better inside and out. The increase of oxygen to the system is something we will discuss in more detail in the next chapter.

I have had many clients who suffered from depression and who, upon beginning an exercise program and sticking with it, found that their depression subsided and that they could see things more clearly and tolerate things more readily.

It may take you several weeks or months to see the significant effects that exercise has on your body. Yet as you exercise and the endorphins in the body are released, the alpha brain waves that cause calming and relaxing effects in our bodies take control, and we begin to feel these calming effects immediately.

When we move our bodies we move our lives. A stagnant body creates a stagnant life. Quit putting off exercising. Find a friend to walk with, or sign up for a yoga or ballet class. If you can't find a friend, exercise by yourself. Callan Pinkney has a great series of videos entitled *Callanetics*. I recommend then highly. Since I have more a dancer's body than an athlete's body, I prefer exercises that lengthen the muscles rather than make them bulky. I feel it's a more feminine look. Consequently, I choose exercise programs that lengthen the muscles, such as yoga or Callenetics.

Whatever exercise you choose to do is not so important. What *is* important is that you get out and do it. Don't waste another minute. Make yourself a promise that you'll start *today* to walk or ride your bike or jog or take yoga or whatever you want to do for at least 15 minutes daily. Then, when you feel up to it, increase this to a half hour, then to forty-five minutes, then to an hour.

Start out three days a week, then increase it to four, then to five, and you may want to increase it to six or seven. But get yourself moving a minimum of three days a week.

No more excuses—start today. *Make the right choice* for a healthy life.

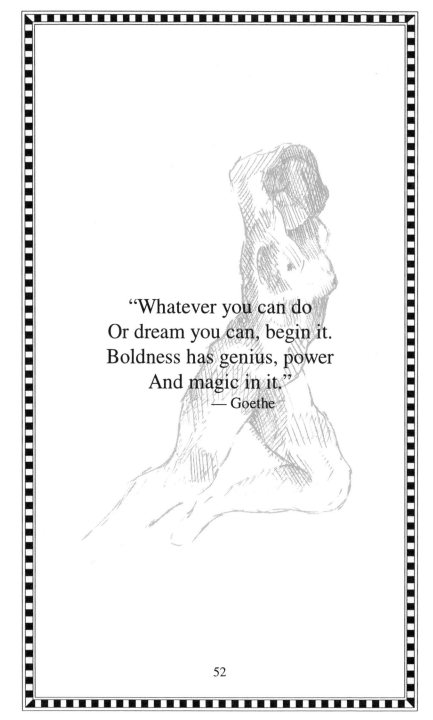

"Whatever you can do
Or dream you can, begin it.
Boldness has genius, power
And magic in it."
— Goethe

# Breathing

As a child, when I was under stress, I would immediately take five to ten deep breaths. I never knew exactly why I was doing this, but I knew it made me feel better and more balanced. As I got older and did more and more research into the mind-body connection, I realized just how important proper breathing is for our good health.

Throughout the years I took lots of breathing lessons, both from my desire to be an opera singer and in my quest for spiritual growth and fulfillment. My vocal coaches would tell me how important it was to breathe properly. They would say that, in order to hold a note and to keep it's tone from going sharp or flat, you had to have "enough air under the note."

They would tell me to hold my hands around my rib cage and expand my diaphragm. When my diaphragm was expanded I was breathing properly. I was told not to raise my chest when I breathed. I always found this to be difficult. It wasn't until years later, when I was taking breathing lessons for the sake of increasing my spiritual awareness, that I was taught an *easy* way to breathe properly.

Lie on your back on the floor. Begin to pay close attention to your breath and what is happening within your body as you're breathing. Notice that you're not raising your chest to breathe, but rather are naturally expanding your diaphragm to hold the air that you've taken in. This is called "diaphragmatic breathing", and is the proper way to breathe. Once you've taken a few breaths and know what it feels like to breathe from the diaphragm instead of the chest, see if you can recreate this standing up. Once you're breathing from the diaphragm rather than the chest, you'll greatly increase your oxygen intake.

This type of breathing is extraordinarily relaxing to the body. It fills the body with much-needed oxygen. It's really the oxygen that releases the endorphins in the body, which give us the sense of peacefulness and calm.

Many believe that breathing properly is the key to preventing disease. The yogis believe that if you breathe deeply you'll never be susceptible to a cold or virus again. In 1931 Dr. Otto Warburg won the Nobel Prize in Medicine for discovering that a lack of oxygen in the body's cells was a prime cause of cancer.

There are many types of healing breathing one can do, but for the purposes of this book, I am going to describe only two—"the cleansing breath" and "pa breathing".

The cleansing breath will help you clean your lungs and respiratory organs. It's a great invigorator if you're feeling tired. You'll find the cleansing breath quite refreshing.

1).     Inhale a complete breath
2).     Retain the air a few seconds
3).     Pucker up the lips as if for a
        whistle (but don't swell out
        the cheeks), then exhale a
        little air through the
        opening, with considerable
        vigor. Then stop for a mo-
        ment, retaining the air, and
        then exhale a little more air.
        Repeat until the air is
        *completely* exhaled. Re-
        member to use considerable
        vigor in exhaling the air
        through the opening in the lips.

Pa breathing is an old yogic internal healing breath, and is wonderful for quickly increasing oxygen to the system. Pa breathing will put the body into an aerobic state all by itself, without putting undo stress on the body.

You begin by bending over and putting your hands on your thighs. Expel all the air you have in your lungs out through your mouth. Quickly inhale a long breath in through your nose and then expel the air from your lungs out through your mouth with the sound of "pa". Hold your stomach in and align your stomach with your internal organs. Hold your breath for the count of 10 and then expel any remaining air through your mouth. It will almost be a sensation of gasping for air. Repeat this for 35 breaths in the morning right after you get up and before you've eaten breakfast, and in the evening just before dinnertime. You want to make sure you're breathing on an empty stomach.

When you first start this breathing technique you may not be able to do 35 breaths. Start out with five and gradually work yourself up to 35. This breathing will oxygenate the blood, and you'll feel more energy almost immediately.

Once you've mastered this ancient yogic breathing exercise, you should get Greer Childers' video entitled *Body Flex*. Greer Childers has literally taken this ancient yogic breathing technique and created a 15- minute exercise program around it. In just 15 minutes a day you can tone and oxygenate your body, and feel better and have more energy in the process.

In her book entitled *Be a Loser* Greer Childers says that "...if you put stress on a particular area of the body...you create a need for more blood to that area. Oxygen is carried to the areas of the body through the blood, and oxygen burns fat..."

Everywhere you turn you hear how important aerobic exercise is. Webster's Dictionary defines the word aerobic as "...increasing the efficiency of oxygen intake by the body." Greer Childers has developed an aerobic breathing program that can literally create an aerobic state through breathing alone.

"Body Flex burns excess body fat (by increasing oxygen to the system, you can utilize or burn eighteen times more fat in your cells than by doing exercise that isn't aerobic) and tones muscle simultaneously with a combination of aerobic breathing and isometric, isotonic and stretch positions."

Oxygen burns fat. If we want to burn excess fat, we have to increase the oxygen levels in our bodies. We increase the oxygen levels by breathing properly.

Deep breathing plays a major role in how we feel. Deep breathing can alleviate all kinds of ailments such as headaches, depression, insomnia, colds, flu, etc. Deep breathing has a calming effect on the body and relieves stress. Proper deep breathing can create such a relaxed state in the body as to lower blood pressure, decrease blood sugar and serum cholesterol levels, improve lung functioning and metabolic rate, improve the digestive process, and more.

The next time you feel stressed out or feel a headache coming on or feel irritable, stop and take ten deep breaths from the diaphragm and see if you don't notice an immediate sensation of relaxation come over you.

It's true that the air we breathe is vital to our health, but so is the way we breathe it. When you breathe deeply you're creating better health for every organ of your body. Shallow breathing causes premature aging. Start breathing properly and you'll find that you have fewer aches and pains, less indigestion and constipation, fewer sore throats and respiratory ailments such as bronchitis, sinus infections, etc. You'll notice that you'll experience more relaxing sleep, and that your complexion is healthier. You'll notice that you have better memory. The list of benefits goes on and on. When you begin breathing deeply and diaphramatically you really will find yourself taking in a breath of fresh air.

# Qualities You Dislike in Others:

1). _____
2). _____
3). _____
4). _____
5). _____
6). _____
7). _____
8). _____
9). _____
10). _____
11). _____
12). _____
13). _____
14). _____
15). _____
16). _____
17). _____
18). _____
19). _____
20). _____

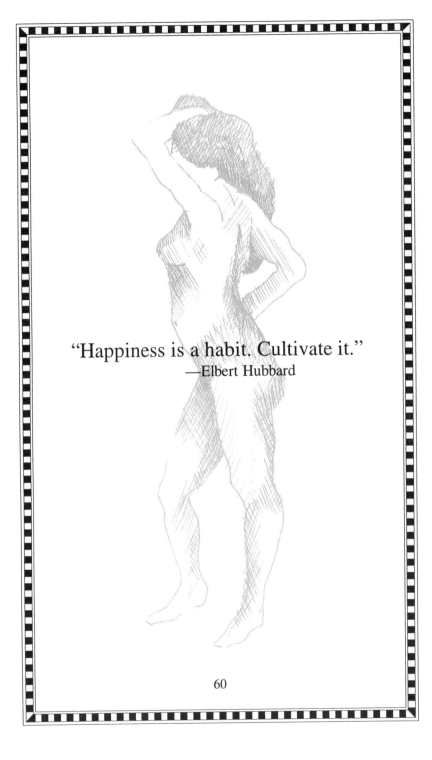

"Happiness is a habit. Cultivate it."
—Elbert Hubbard

# Aromatherapy

The sense of smell is probably the most lightly regarded of the senses, yet aromas have amazing influence over us. We can be instantly brought back to a moment in time of intense pleasure or pain merely by smelling the same scent that was present at the original moment. The sense of smell has the ability to arouse an instant emotional response in us, be it good or bad.

Aromas can relax us, energize us, get us in the mood for lovemaking, make us feel safe (or threatened), remind us of spending cold winter weekends at Grandma's house waiting for the home-made pie to be ready for eating. In fact, much of the pleasure we derive from food is a direct result of the food's aroma.

We are drawn to some people and repelled by others because of our sense of smell. Smells can warn us of impending danger. There is no question that an aroma creates an instant emotional response. This response may be a result of something from the past or it may be a scent that you instinctively like or dislike. There is no question that the sense of smell is extremely important.

At Blueberry Hill, we teach our clients about the positive impact that different aromas can have on our bodies and senses. We incorporate various aromas into the program to help relax our clients during meditation or relaxation periods, to energize our clients during exercise periods, to clear the mind during teaching periods. We use aromas to help stimulate the metabolic process while we're eating, to alleviate depression, and for many other purposes.

Since aromas can help to intensify our experiences, when we wish to recreate such an experience we can do so merely by introducing the proper aroma into our surroundings. We use aromas in several ways. We place a scented oil on a ring around a light in the room or rooms that one of our clients is going to be in. We choose the oil according to the desired result.

We use aromatherapy during massage. If the masseuse is giving a deep tissue massage (this will be described later) she may use a more stimulating aromatic oil. If she is giving a relaxing massage she will use an aromatic oil known to be relaxing.

We also use aromatherapy oils in the bath. Regardless of whether we're trying to invigorate or relax the body, the oils are a quick and easy way to do so. Here is a list of some of our favorite scents and the effects they have come to be associated with.

| | |
|---|---|
| Amber | Healing, Uplifting |
| Benzoin | Energizing, Stimulating |
| Bergamot | Anti-depressant |
| Bitter Orange | Raises one's spirits |

| | |
|---|---|
| Cedar | Purification |
| Chamomile | Calming, Relaxing |
| Cinnamon | Stimulating |
| Cypress | Sedative, Soothing |
| Eucalyptus | Clears the mind |
| Frankincense | Purification |
| Gardenia | Aphrodisiac, Love |
| Geranium | Uplifting |
| Grapefruit | Soothing |
| Honeysuckle | Concentration |
| Jasmine | Relaxation |
| Lavender | Relaxation |
| Lemon | Refreshes, Clears |
| Lime | Stimulating |
| Myrrh | Healing, Peace |
| Mandarin | Good for skin |
| Patchouli | Stimulating |
| Peppermint | Stimulating |
| Pine | Stimulating |
| Rose | Love, Calming |
| Rosemary | Clears the mind |
| Sage | Uplifting |
| Sandalwood | Uplifting |
| Sweet Marjoram | Calming |
| Tea Tree | Powerful antiseptic |
| Vanilla | Soothing, Healing |
| Violet | Healing, Stimulating |
| Ylang, Ylang | Good for insomnia |

These are but a few of the aromas available in the marketplace today. My all time favorite aromatherapy oil is lavender. I use lavender for so many things here at Blueberry Hill. If someone arrives stressed, I immediately put the lavender oil on the light bulb rings and within minutes the person is calm and relaxed.

I find lavender to be one of the most versatile and relaxing oils, not to mention one of the most healing. Lavender is uplifting and soothing. It alleviates stress, depression, insomnia, headaches and muscle aches, among other conditions.

Another oil we use quite a bit here at Blueberry Hill is peppermint. We use it for our foot and hand massages. It's both stimulating and strengthening, and uplifts the entire system. It possesses antispasmodic qualities as well. It's very invigorating and soothing for tired hands and feet. It's very cooling and counteracts fatigue.

When we're teaching our clients we use the scent of lemon, to help clear the mind so that it can retain the knowledge it's absorbing. Lemon is a clean, fresh scent that makes people happy.

To create an aromatherapy bath, run your bath water, adding a particular scent depending on the effect you'd like to achieve. If you want to relax the body I would suggest lavender or chamomile. Just before you get into the tub, pour in 5-6 drops of the selected oil. It will float on top of the water, and with the warm water will be absorbed into your skin. Simultaneously, you'll be inhaling the scent, which will be both psychologically and physiologically beneficial.

A great evening bath we draw for our clients at Blueberry Hill is a combination of 3 drops lavender and 2 drops ylang,ylang. This bath is great for total relaxation after a long hard day.

You can also make your own bath salts using aromatherapy oils. Get a box of Epsom Salts, a bottle of glycerin, your favorite aromatherapy oil (again I suggest lavender), and food coloring. Combine 2 cups of Epsom Salts, a teaspoon of glycerin, 1-2 drops of food coloring and 7-10 drops of your favorite aromatherapy oil. Mix in a big bowl with a spoon, and when it's completely blended seal in an airtight container. You now have some great inexpensive bath salts which will smell—and feel—wonderful.

Moods can be enhanced—or changed entirely—with the use of aromas. There's no doubt about it—aroma-therapy is a gentle, easy, simple and highly effective way to relieve stress and anxiety, and markedly raise the quality of your everyday life.

"Too many people overvalue
what they're not and undervalue
what they are."
—Malcomb Forbes

# Eating Right

Is it true, as Adelle Davis said, that we are what we eat? Or might it be even *more* true to say that we are what we *think* about when we're eating?

It's undeniable that diet plays a very important part in our overall health, for good *or* ill. In fact, many doctors are beginning to realize that what we ingest can often be *hazardous* to our health.

Beyond the obvious advice (eat more fresh foods and fewer processed ones, etc.), I can't tell you what you should be eating, because everyone is different. Some have meat-eating constitutions. Their bodies crave a lot of protein, especially red meat. Others need more carbohydrates to create energy in their bodies. Still others have a lighter constitution and require more fruits and vegetables in their diet.

You probably know instinctively what kind of food *you* prefer to eat. If you eat a lot of meat and feel energized after doing so, you know you're a meat eater. Those of us who feel sleepy and sluggish after eating red meat know that we can consume meat occasionally, but that it should not be our primary food.

I have a much lighter digestive system. I feel my best when I eat fruits, vegetables, and whole grains. When I eat a lot of red meat I feel very tired and sluggish. I feel as though I need a nap. The same is true if I eat a lot of potatoes. These heavier foods are just too much for me. I like them and I eat them on occasion, but I try to limit my intake of them so that I feel my best.

No matter what type of food you like to eat, the key to eating a healthy meal is to make sure you're eating healthy, fresh foods. Make sure you're washing your foods well so that you're not ingesting any pesticides. When possible, buy organic fruits and vegetables. It may cost a little more money up front, but you'll save a lot in doctor's bills.

We've all heard that we should try to limit our intake of sugar and avoid foods that aren't "real", such as sugar substitutes. We've heard we should avoid pre-made or pre-cooked frozen foods, as well as most canned and fat-free foods since they're both usually high in sodium. We've been encouraged to eliminate all soft drinks from our diet and to drink more water.

None of this is new information by any means. So why then aren't we paying more attention to the foods we eat? Well, for starters we're all in such a hurry to live our lives. Everything is done on the run. It's unusual these days for most people to sit down and eat a meal with their families. Many of us don't even take the time to eat a relaxed meal *alone*.

While most of the medical community would

like you to believe that you won't be healthy if you eat spicy foods, fatty foods, sweet foods, deep fried foods, etc., the truth is that people all over the world are eating these types of foods and feeling just fine. The French consume huge amounts of fat in the sauces they eat, yet they have almost no heart disease. How can this be?

Well, what if our health has less than we've thought to do with *what* we eat, and a lot more to do with what we *think* about when we're eating? What if you could eat a hot fudge sundae and not gain weight? What if you could actually become healthy while eating foods that aren't supposed to be particularly healthy for you?

I believe that, in large measure, your body will derive just about as much—or as little—benefit from the food you eat as your mind and your attitude have *prepared* your body to derive.

If you're eating a hot fudge sundae, for example, and you're thinking that this food is nutritious and will provide your body with the nutrients it needs to create the energy you want, I believe this hot fudge sundae is going to be downright good for you.

Conversely, if you're eating a salad, and while you're doing it you're berating yourself because you're eating so much, telling yourself that you're disgusting for eating the entire salad, etc., I believe this salad has just lost much of it's nutritional value for you. You've literally imbued the food with negativity, and now you're not only thinking negative thoughts but you're ingesting negativity as well.

It's vital that we be conscious and aware while we're eating—of the food itself, the benefits the food is providing us, and the positive feelings we have about the taste of the food, the nutrition the food is giving us, and how much we're enjoying eating it.

At Blueberry Hill we teach women to be conscious about what they're eating, *and* what they're thinking about *while* they're eating. We teach them to create a mantra they can play over and over in their minds while they're eating. That mantra may be something like, "I am beautiful and strong" or "I am vibrant and healthy" or "I love myself and provide myself with all good things." I'm sure you get the idea.

We teach our clients *how* to eat a healthy meal, which we feel is just as important as the meal itself. One thing I teach women is *never* to eat in their cars. *Never, never, never* eat in your car. When we eat on the run we *can't* be completely conscious of what we're eating. Also, we tend to eat more junk food when we eat in our cars. Since we're usually in a hurry when we order from a drive through window at a fast food place, we're naturally eating our food with the same haste. This is not conscious eating, and it's not healthy eating. Here are what I call the "5 Rules for Healthy Eating":

Rule #1 -    No eating in your car.

|  |  |
|---|---|
| | Never. Period. |
| Rule #2 - | You must sit down to eat. Again, this is so you can be conscious of your meal, and relaxed while you eat it. |
| Rule #3 - | Bless your food. Be grateful for the food you're about to eat. This is an old custom and a marvelous one. When we bless the food and show gratitude we're helping to create a truly healthy meal for ourselves, spiritually and psychologically as well as physically. |
| Rule #4 - | Verbalize exactly what you intend the food to do for you. For example, "This hamburger is going to give me all the nutrition I need to create the energy in my body to complete my daily work. It tastes fabulous and I enjoy every bite." |
| Rule #5 - | Then, while you're eating your meal, repeat your mantra in your mind. |

If you're having breakfast, lunch or dinner with a family member or friend, make certain that your conversation is positive and uplifting. *Don't* discuss horrors at the dinner table. Mealtime is not the time to talk about the latest killings in Bosnia, or the recent passing of a friend or relative. This is not the time to watch television, either. Remember to be consciously aware of the food you're eating and the thoughts you're having while you eat it, and you'll be imbuing your food with positive attributes that will create a more healthy body, mind and spirit.

Pay attention to the *reason* you're eating. Are you really physically hungry for food, or are you trying to feed emotional, mental or spiritual hungers with that food? When you become conscious of *why* you're eating and what hungers you're trying to feed, you can then feed your *nutritional* hunger with food, and find other, more satisfying and appropriate ways to feed your emotional, mental and spiritual hungers.

Imagine you find yourself making a sandwich, and you ask yourself, "Am I *really* experiencing nutritional hunger?" Let's say you find that the answer is no, that you're really experiencing a need for love or companionship. Because you're now consciously aware of the real nature of the hunger you're experiencing, you can put the sandwich away and call a friend to go to a movie, or begin to volunteer some time to a cause close to your heart.

You'll be amazed at how good you feel, how many new friends you'll make, and how your emotional hunger will be satisfied.

In 1970, at Ohio State University in Columbus, Ohio, medical researchers conducted a study of heart disease. Rabbits were fed extremely toxic, high cholesterol diets to see if, as in humans, the rabbits' arteries would become blocked. As you might imagine, the results did indeed show that this toxic diet was blocking the rabbits' arteries—in all test groups but one. The one group, in fact, showed 60 percent fewer symptoms than the other groups.

The researchers conducting the study couldn't find anything at all to account for this group's good health despite such a toxic diet. In fact, they believed that perhaps these rabbits were not really being given the toxic food. The researchers paid a surprise visit to the student in charge of this healthy group of rabbits and discovered something amazing. The rabbits were indeed being fed this high cholesterol diet; but the student was an animal lover, and just prior to feeding them this toxic food, he would hold them and pet them and tell them how lovely they were.

That's *right!* Love was literally the difference in this study. The rabbits that felt loved had no adverse reaction to the toxic food. This is true of us as well. When we feel loved we eat just what's right for us; and the food we eat seems to do us more good than it might otherwise be expected to.

That's what I call a healthy development.

When we eat, we need to make certain that we're creating a loving environment for ourselves. This is so important because we're affecting and energizing our bodies on many levels when we eat. Do little things like setting a beautiful table for yourself, arranging some fresh cut flowers for the table, and eating by soft candlelight. Make certain that you're playing relaxing music in the background. There's nothing more annoying (or more likely to cause indigestion) than eating food to a rock beat.

Be conscious of, and grateful for, what you're eating—be loving and gentle with yourself—and begin to feel what it's like to experience a meal as it *should* be experienced. You'll be delighted with all the wonderful sensations, and you'll be amazed at all the benefits.

# Qualities You Look for in a Friend:

1). _____
2). _____
3). _____
4). _____
5). _____
6). _____
7). _____
8). _____
9). _____
10). _____
11). _____
12). _____
13). _____
14). _____
15). _____
16). _____
17). _____
18). _____
19). _____
20). _____

"You're what you are, and you're where you are, because of what's gone into your mind. You can change what you are, and you can change where you are, by changing what goes into your mind."
—Zig Ziglar

# Meditation

Meditation is one of the most rewarding things you can do for yourself. It's a practice that goes back many centuries, and has been effectively used in countless cultures. Many people are confused about how to meditate, but it's really quite simple once you get the hang of it.

Meditation is literally just quieting the chatter in the mind. Sounds easy, right? But sometimes, in this hectic world we live in, it's easier said than done. Since the simple act of quieting the mind has so many benefits for the body, mind and spirit, it just makes sense that it should become an essential part of your day.

The opportunity to connect with "a higher power", a greater part of ourselves, or whatever you wish to call it, seems to bring everything into perspective. It's truly amazing how calming and peaceful the process is. When I'm under a lot of stress, I just take several deep breaths in through the nose and exhale out through the mouth, relax my body (I'll explain the technique), and begin to meditate for 15-20 minutes, stilling my thoughts and asking for guidance. Benefits are nearly always immediate.

Meditation has been used to reduce stress, relax the body, create increased mental clarity, and prepare oneself for more focused prayer. In meditation the brain waves go into what is called an alpha state. This is the brain wave state in which the body is completely relaxed while the mind remains alert. It's "in alpha" that many writers write, artists paint, and composers create their music.

Alpha waves are the brain waves associated with relaxation and receptive states of mind. If you were to look at an electroencephalogram (EEG) of a person's alpha waves while they slept, and then see the EEG of the same person's alpha waves during meditation, you would see that the alpha waves created through meditation have a far greater intensity than those produced during sleep. You would also see that the level of relaxation achieved is much greater during meditation than during sleep. There's also a more complete synchronization between the right and left hemispheres of the brain during meditation.

In the late 1960s Dr. Keith Wallace at the University of California found in his research studies that while the body became more relaxed during meditation, the mind actually became more *alert*. Results of many other clinical studies have shown that meditation reduces anxiety, depression, pain, headaches, insomnia, and more. Meditation can literally help keep you healthy.

So how do you meditate? Well, you can meditate lying down, sitting cross legged on the floor, or sitting in a comfortable chair. At Blueberry Hill we teach our clients to meditate sitting in a comfortable chair, since we don't want them to fall asleep.

Wear comfortable clothes. Sit with your back erect, arms uncrossed with hands on tops of thighs and palms facing up. Legs should be uncrossed with feet flat on the floor. Close your eyes. Start by taking in several deep breaths through the nose and exhaling the breaths through the mouth.

Focus your attention on your breathing. Imagine that you are inhaling love, light, joy, and perfect health, and that you are exhaling tension, anxiety, ill health and all fear. Inhale the positives and exhale the negatives for ten to twelve deep breaths. Now start at your feet and begin to tense every part of your body and then relax it. First tense your toes. Relax your toes. Tense your feet. Relax your feet. Tense your calves. Relax your calves. Then repeat the process with your thighs, your stomach, your torso, your fingers, your hands, your forearms, your upper arms, your shoulders, your back, your neck muscles, your facial muscles, your forehead, and finally, tense your entire body at once and then relax your entire body. You are now ready for meditation. (Incidentally, this is also a terrific way to prepare for sleep.)

Repeat this phrase over and over to yourself, concentrating fully on it: "God, my heart is open to you. Come into my heart." You'll begin to feel a sense of peace come over you. When you become aware of this, begin your mantra. For example: "God, my heart is open to you. Come into my heart and show me my beauty," or, "God, my heart is open to you. Come into my heart and help me to feel loved." Whatever it is that you desire, repeat it over and over as your mantra.

Try to do this for at least 15-20 minutes a day. You'll see the most profound experiences if you meditate at least twice a day.

Meditation will relax you, help you to cope with stressful situations and relationships in your life, create better overall health and well being, and release the body tension that makes us age.

# List Your Top 20 Accomplishments:

1). _____
2). _____
3). _____
4). _____
5). _____
6). _____
7). _____
8). _____
9). _____
10). _____
11). _____
12). _____
13). _____
14). _____
15). _____
16). _____
17). _____
18). _____
19). _____
20). _____

"See the possibilities."
—Norman Vincent Peal

# Visualization

Visualization is a technique which uses a person's own imagination to create an outcome. You may want to achieve greater success in life, create better health, cope with stress, ace a test, give a great speech, etc. All these can be done more readily using visualization. Many successful athletes use visualization techniques to prepare them for their contests.

Your subconscious does not really know the difference between an actual and an imagined event. It automatically reacts to information which you feed it—information you believe to be accurate. Dr. Maxwell Maltz in his landmark book *Psycho-Cybernetics* states: "You act, and feel, not ac-cording to what things are really like, but according to the image your mind holds of what they are like. You have certain mental images of yourself, your world, and the people around you, and you behave as though these images were the truth, the reality, rather than the things they represent."

Maltz further writes, "If we picture ourselves performing in a certain manner, it's nearly the same as the actual performance. Mental practice makes perfect." Maltz goes on to cite several studies in which creative visualization is used. One experiment was conducted to see if the use of visualization could improve the skills of basketball players sinking free throws.

The study lasted 20 days. During that period, students of equal ability were divided into three groups. They were all tested on the first day of the study and the last day of the study. The first group physically practiced free throwing for 20 minutes every day for 20 consecutive days, and at the end of the 20 days they had improved by 24%. The second group engaged in no sort of practice whatsoever during the 20 days, and at the end they showed no improvement. The third group spent 20 minutes every day for 20 consecutive days *imagining* themselves sinking the free throws—in other words, practicing in their minds eye. If they missed a shot, they would imagine themselves making the correction in technique and sinking the free throw. At the end of the 20 days, this group had improved by 23%—virtually as much improvement as those who had actually thrown the ball.

A psychologist by the name of R. A. Vandell demonstrated that mental practice in throwing darts improved aim as much as actually throwing the darts. Many noted golfers have used visualization. Ben Hogan, Johnny Bulla, and most recently Tiger Woods have all declared that they use visualization. In an interview with Sports Illustrated, Tiger Woods spoke of how he would imagine or visualize himself hitting the ball to the hole. He would imagine every aspect of his shot. We all know what a superb young golfer Tiger Woods is today.

More and more athletes proudly proclaim

that they use visualization techniques to practice their skills. Several Olympic gold medal champions have actually hired visualization trainers to help them mentally prepare for their competitions. Visualization seems to stimulate the right hemisphere of the brain, where emotions and creativity take place. The visual part of the cerebral cortex is activated by imagery involving sight. The auditory cortex is triggered by sound imagery, and the sensory cortex is triggered by imagery involving touch. The key to visualization is to make sure that you *feel* it—that you *believe* it's true while you are imagining it. Experience indicates that if you repeat the visualization enough, you actually begin to believe it and act as if the image were true.

At Blueberry Hill we teach our clients to visualize themselves becoming more healthy, more confident, more happy and joy filled. We have them visualize healthier, happier, more fulfilling relationships for themselves, as well as greater successes in all areas of their lives.

So how do we visualize? We relax our bodies as described in the previous chapter on meditation. Then we picture something we want. Perhaps we're about to go on a job interview for a new position. We imagine the entire interview in our mind's eye. We imagine the questions being asked of us and our responses to the questions. We imagine the entire process over and over in our mind, always with a very favorable outcome. And most important, we believe that the outcome we're imagining is not only possible but is *true* at the moment we're visualizing it.

It's important to realize that visualization helps us to be the best we can be. It cannot be used to manipulate or control others. It will give you the edge you need to be the best you can be in any given situation, and allow others to see you at your best, and base their decisions about you on that best impression.

# List 20 Goals:

1). _____
2). _____
3). _____
4). _____
5). _____
6). _____
7). _____
8). _____
9). _____
10). _____
11). _____
12). _____
13). _____
14). _____
15). _____
16). _____
17). _____
18). _____
19). _____
20). _____

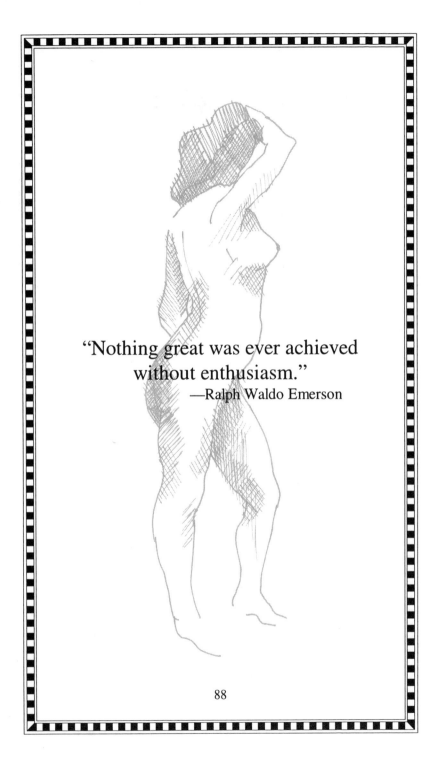

"Nothing great was ever achieved
without enthusiasm."
—Ralph Waldo Emerson

# Music and Sound

When I was a child I was intrigued with sound, and the effects it had on people. While most of my friends were listening to rock and roll, I was listening to opera and classical music. I realized that certain music was extremely relaxing, while other music was downright nerve-jangling, even sometimes irritating.

I loved music, and could often be heard telling others about the healing properties of sound. People generally just nodded and smiled when I spoke of how sound would one day play a major part in healing. After all, I was a child, and while everyone knew music could evoke a wide range of emotions, there was nothing concrete to indicate it could ever be used in any real medicinal way.

But times do change. Today music and sound are regular topics in our medical journals. For example, Alzheimer patients who are no longer able to speak are able to sing songs they learned as children. Why? It's now known that the part of the brain which deals with music is the last part of the brain to be affected by age or disease.

We also now know that certain types of music can stimulate specific areas of the brain, creating such results as relaxation, improved memory and mental focus, increased creativity, etc. *The Mozart Effect* by Don Campbell describes how Mozart's music can literally amplify the learning processes.

The effects of music on the immune system are being studied around the world. Medical studies conducted in the United States, Germany, and England indicate that patients who listen to certain types of music actually made faster recoveries, with less anxiety and discomfort.

In Germany, studies conducted by Dr. Ralph Spintge found that one could lower one's heart rate, blood pressure and respiration, thereby lowering stress levels, just by playing music with a certain rhythm. Music is truly a Universal language.

Composers from the 17th and 18th centuries— especially the Baroque Period—incorporated certain harmonics into their music. It now seems that these harmonics have powerful healing properties. The neurons of the brain seem to resonate with these harmonics and create a heightened sense of well-being.

Dr. Georgi Lozanov, a Bulgarian physician and psychologist, used the music of these 17th and 18th century composers in the learning system he created and called *Suggestopedia*. Lozanov studied the Baroque composers and found that the largo movements of their music helped create a meditative state. These largo movements were written to be played at 55-60 beats a minute, which was about the same as the normal tempo of the relaxed heart. Playing music with this tempo literally slowed the heart rate, relaxing the body yet leaving the mind alert.

Lozanov's next step was to study the effects of rhythm on learning. He discovered that the maximum amount of information would be retained if it was delivered in a cadence of 8-second increments. We'll discuss this further when we get to the chapter on how to re-program the subconscious mind. By combining the largo movements of Baroque music with information repeated three times in 8-second cadences, he found that people learned information from two to ten times faster than normal, with an extra-ordinarily high retention rate. His program, *Suggestopedia*, was born.

In France, Dr. Alfred Tomatis, an ear, nose and throat specialist, was studying the effects of sound frequencies. He found that what we hear plays an important part in our health. He also found that children can hear even before they are born, and that this pre-natal auditory experience was extremely important in a child's development. He found that high frequency sounds are quite beneficial and provide us with added energy, while low frequency sounds—like the every day noises of traffic, most office machines, jack hammers, computers, etc.—literally sap the energy right out of our bodies.

Dr. Tomatis found that certain music, particularly Mozart, could help people overcome developmental problems, including learning disabilities and other disorders. Dr. Tomatis would often say that "Mozart is an excellent mother."

A research study conducted in the early 1990s

at the University of California, Irvine, by Drs. Gordon Shaw and Frances Rauscher, found that listening to Mozart for 10 minutes prior to taking a test greatly enhanced spatial intelligence (an important component of IQ). New technology enables us actually to take a look inside the brain; and researchers using these new techniques have found that listening to music affects our sense of "time, space and overall perception."

Dr. Tomatis found that the language centers of the brain could be stimulated by high frequencies. Tomatis said "Mozart charges the brain", allowing for more reception and retention by the listener. Mozart's music is literally an exercise program for the ear—and for the brain.

No two people hear sounds in precisely the same way, since different people's ears are slightly different, and each of us listens and hears sounds in each ear a little differently. Not only is sound subtly different for each of us, but it also differs for each of us depending on the time of day, the amount of sleep we've had, our stress levels, and numerous other factors.

Sound is measured in both frequencies and decibels. Frequencies are a measure of tones, and decibels are a measure of how loud the sound is. High frequencies and low decibels are healing, and low frequencies and high decibels can create illness, loss of hearing, nervous disorders, and other problems.

Dr. Tomatis invented a system which allows

one to listen to music with the lower frequencies filtered out and the higher frequencies enhanced. His system has been extremely beneficial for those with learning disabilities (including dyslexia) and autism. His system has also been extremely helpful in treating tinnitis (or "ringing in the ears").

Everyone and everything in the Universe vibrates at a certain ideal frequency. If you have two violins tuned to the same pitch, and you pluck a string on one of the violins, the violin you pluck will send out a sound frequency which will vibrate the matching string on the second violin, causing it to produce the same tone. This is called "resonance", and we all experience it on a daily basis. When you meet someone for the first time, you often feel you are "resonating" with them. (We used to call this "good vibes".) The law of resonance affects us at many levels—physical, emotional, mental, and spiritual.

Everything vibrates at a particular frequency—everything. Each and every one of us is vibrating at a certain frequency. When we're vibrating at our normal rate we're healthy. But when we allow stress, limiting beliefs, fear, lack of proper nutrition, lack of sleep, etc. to enter our lives, we lower our vibratory rate and create illness. And when one part of our body lowers its vibratory rate, it lowers the vibratory rate of the entire body.

When this happens, we need to remind the dysfunctional part of the body what its true frequency is, so it can repair itself, increase its vibration, and return the body to its natural balance. We can achieve this by sending a message in the form of a frequency to the dysfunctional body part. Fortunately, we can consciously choose to increase our vibratory rates.

Each organ of our body vibrates at its own frequency as well, and when an organ becomes out of balance its frequency is lowered, creating disease within that particular organ and within the body as a whole. You can bring each individual organ back to its natural balance—and the entire body back to a healthy state—by playing the frequencies that are associated with the organ when it's healthy.

At Blueberry Hill we work a lot with sound and music therapy. We use the work of Nicole La-Voie called Sound Wave Energy (SWE). Nicole has created more than forty sound frequency tapes which can be used for everything from relaxing the body to creating more clarity and focus in one's life, to bringing the body into balance naturally, to increasing oxygen to the cells, to manifesting your heart's desire, increasing circulation, increasing feelings of well being, creating better hearing, and a number of other desired results.

We specifically use the tapes to open up the *chakra* (energy) centers of the body, to bring the body into its own perfect balance. We play these frequencies under the sound of Baroque music or Mozart, depending on what we're trying to accomplish.

When we're teaching or doing healing work,

we'll play one of a number of Mozart pieces available on the CD *Music for the Mozart Effect*, from Don Campbell. If we're trying to create a relaxing environment for meditation or visualization, we'll play the largo movements of Baroque composers such as Vivaldi, Telemann, Bach, Handel and others. Underneath these pieces we'll be playing SWE frequencies to optimize a person's balance and normal good health.

As Congreve wrote more than 300 years ago, "Music has charms to soothe a savage breast." Today we know its powers are broader by far. For your own benefit, I encourage you to sing or hum as often as possible. Begin to train your ears to the higher frequencies. You are literally stimulating your brain and creating a healthier mind and body in the process.

"Happiness doesn't depend upon who you are or what you have; it depends upon what you think."
—Dale Carnegie

# Massage

The skin is the body's largest organ, and its primary sensory organ. It's through the skin that all sense of touch is perceived. The sense of touch is the first sense to develop in the embryo. Since humans are very social creatures, you don't have to be terribly perceptive to see that a baby thrives with positive touch, especially its mother's.

By touching we send messages through the nervous system to the brain. Gentle touch or massage can release the body's natural endorphins and create a state of relaxation and overall well-being. A more vigorous massage may remove tension from the muscles, reducing discomfort and producing more flexibility.

Massage is great for relaxing the body, stimulating it, or both simultaneously, depending on the type of massage you get. Massage can have a direct effect on your heart rate, blood pressure, digestion, breathing, etc. It's quite effective in reducing stress levels in the body, because it can literally lower the amount of circulating stress hormones, such as cortisol and norepinephrine, which can weaken the immune system.

Massage enhances skin tone by supplying more oxygen and nutrients to the body tissues. And massage is extremely useful in removing toxins from the body. Lactic acid and other chemical wastes, which can lead to stiffness and pain in the joints and muscles, are eliminated through massage.

Touch is important for all of us. You've probably heard that it takes a certain number of hugs a day to be healthy. At the Touch Research Institute (TRI), University of Miami School of Medicine, a study was conducted on premature babies. Those premature babies who were lovingly touched daily were more active, gained 47% more weight, and were able to leave the hospital six days earlier on average than babies who weren't lovingly touched.

TRI further found that teenagers with anorexia and bulimia had a better body image and less depression after massage, that HIV positive men produced more of the cells that destroy bacteria and viruses when massaged daily, that children with asthma suffered fewer asthmatic attacks when massaged, that glucose levels fell to normal in diabetic children after four weeks of massage. The research is ongoing, and the discoveries just keep coming.

At Blueberry Hill clients have 3 to 5 massages over the five-day period. The massages last for an hour-and-a-half and are administered at various times of the day depending on the type of massage. Regardless of massage type, however, everyone must consume at least 8 glasses of water a day when they have a massage.

A massage releases so many toxins that you want to make sure that you're consuming enough water to flush the toxins from your system. This is very important. In fact, many experts now recommend the 8 glasses a day as a regular practice.

"Never mistake motion for action."
—Ernest Hemingway

# Reflexology

Many believe that deep relaxation and healing can be achieved by massaging the feet and or hands. This form of massage is known as "reflexology", and we use it here at Blueberry Hill. In common with many who practice Oriental medicine, reflexologists believe that the hands and feet are mirrors of the body, that each organ of the body has a corresponding point on the hands and the feet, and that by applying pressure to these areas we can stimulate healing directly in those areas.

There are roughly 7,200 nerve endings in each foot. Massaging the feet brings better circulation, and carries more oxygen and nutrients to the body, helping to remove toxins. It's believed that waste products such as calcium crystals and uric acid actually accumulate around the various reflex points in the hands and feet, and that massaging the hands and/or feet can remove them by promoting freer flowing of the blood, which carries these toxins out of the system.

Dr. William H. Fitzgerald believed that the zones on the left side of the body related to the reflex points on the left hand and foot, and that the zones on the right side of the body related to the reflex points on the right hand and foot. He called his theory The Zone Theory. What we now know as reflexology was subsequently developed by

Eunice Ingham. She took Dr. Fitzgerald's theory and took it a step further, creating a "map" of the feet and the hands showing the pressure points that relate to the various parts of the body.

Reflexologists believe that granular or crystalline deposits will accumulate on the applicable reflex point, making it feel sensitive to the touch, when there is an imbalance in the body. The more sensitive the area is to the touch, the greater the imbalance in the body. External manifestations of problems in the body can take the form of hard skin, corns, bunions, or infections.

Even a person's state of mind is said to have a correlating reflex point in both the feet and hands, and as a consequence it's believed that in many instances emotional problems as well may respond to this type of therapy. Reflexology definitely seems to work well for stress-related disorders, headaches, tension, constipation, and more. We use it at Blueberry Hill to help our clients restore an overall sense of good health.

# *People and Things You Love:*

1). _____
2). _____
3). _____
4). _____
5). _____
6). _____
7). _____
8). _____
9). _____
10). _____
11). _____
12). _____
13). _____
14). _____
15). _____
16). _____
17). _____
18). _____
19). _____
20). _____

"Quit worrying about your health.
It'll go away."
—Robert Orben

# Healing Therapies

At Blueberry Hill we provide a wide range of therapies for our clients. While we have discussed many of them in some detail, there are three others we use to a somewhat lesser degree. Nevertheless, we consider them important.

## Magnetic Therapy

The earth has its own magnetic field, aligned to the north and south poles. Our own body cells have subtle magnetic fields as well. Electromagnetic fields (EMFs) are everywhere. Electrical equipment that generates EMFs is used in conventional medicine to sway the body's natural electric currents in the direction of healing. There are many practitioners who believe that ordinary magnets are capable of doing the same thing, and who use magnetic mattresses, wrist bands, braces and wraps to treat illness or imbalance in the body.

Supposedly, magnets are able to stimulate the iron atoms in the red corpuscles of the blood. When a magnet is placed on the body, blood flow to that area of the body is increased, improving the supply of oxygen to the cells. This stimulates the metabolism and aids in eliminating waste products.

Magnets are said to be good for many things. Many practitioners believe that if you magnetize water by placing it on the negative pole of a magnet for up to 24 hours, drinking that water will aid your digestion. Magnetic insoles for your shoes are believed to emit small magnetic charges which improve circulation, energy, and endurance. I have never tried these, but my father uses them and claims to notice the difference. Believe me when I tell you my father is the King of the Skeptics, so if he notices a difference there really *is* a difference. Magnets may be worn on the knees, elbows, ankles, wrists, lower back—in fact anywhere one is experiencing muscle pain or discomfort. Many who experience the muscular pain associated with arthritis and rheumatoid arthritis swear by their magnets.

At Blueberry Hill our clients sleep on magnetic mattress pads which recharge the body, stimulate the immune system, and improve circulation. The negative pole of the mattress pad is calming and promotes a restful sound sleep. I have been sleeping on one for several months now, and really didn't notice a difference until I went away on business and came back to my heavenly mattress. One caution—they should not be used by anyone who is pregnant, trying to conceive, or has a pacemaker.

# Art Therapy

At Blueberry Hill we believe it's important to stay in touch with that part of us which is innocent and childlike. To that end we use art as our means of expression. One of my favorite exercises to share with clients, and to have them share with me, is the creation of a treasure map.

They start out with a piece of poster board, a pair of scissors, a glue stick, and some old magazines. They decide what they would like to create in their lives, and then go through the magazines to find the pictures which depict what it is they want. They cut out the pictures and paste them on the poster board, creating a collage of sorts.

This collage is very powerful for several reasons. First, it was created in childlike fun, so all those feelings are transferred to the treasure map. Second, the client takes this map and places it where she will see it every day. This becomes a constant visual reminder of what she is trying to achieve. By taking a few moments first thing in the morning and just before bedtime to concentrate on her treasure map, and imagine herself having whatever she has created on that map, she sends a signal to her subconscious mind to go get it.

Art therapy is a wonderful, simple, refreshingly childlike way to find the natural, easy solution to the problem at hand.

# Color Therapy

You've no doubt read or seen on television that our bodies have an "aura", or energy field, that displays colors. This aura reflects the state of our health through the colors it emits.

Light travels in waves. Our brains perceive its varying wavelengths as different colors. Like each of us, each color has its own frequency, which correlates with the rate at which it vibrates. We know that color can affect our mood, but it also has healing properties based upon its frequency.

When full spectrum light travels through a prism it refracts, or separates, into red, orange, yellow, green, blue, indigo and violet—the seven colors of the spectrum. These colors also correspond with the seven energy centers (chakras) of the physical body. Here are the significant characteristics of the colors:

Red is associated with the first chakra, located at the base of the coccyx. It affects the adrenal glands and relieves inertia. It can create courage, physical energy and vitality.

Orange is associated with the second chakra, located in the lower abdomen. It affects the reproductive organs and relieves depression. It can create happiness, optimism and sexual energy.

Yellow is associated with the third chakra, located in the solar plexus. This chakra is the seat of all our emotions. It affects the pancreas and relieves unresolved feelings. It can create determination.

Green is associated with the fourth chakra, located in the heart. It affects the thymus gland and relieves nervous tension. It can create freedom, balance, harmony, sympathy and love.

Blue is associated with the fifth chakra, located in the throat. It affects the thyroid gland and relieves insomnia and overactivity. It can create inspiration, peace, creativity, relaxation, devotion and trust.

Violet is associated with the sixth chakra, located in the forehead. It affects the pituitary gland and relieves addiction. It can create perception, intuition, self-respect and tolerance.

Magenta is associated with the seventh chakra, located at the crown of the head. It affects the pineal gland and relieves compulsive behavior. It can create spiritual development, reverence, commitment and idealism.

When one of the energy centers of the body is out of balance, we can bring it back into balance by using the appropriate color and its complimentary opposite. The use of color can help to correct any imbalances in the body and create a state of harmony.

Color research has found yellow and red to be the most stimulating colors, and blue and black to be the most calming. Yellow has been found to increase one's learning ability. Red can cause your heart rate and blood pressure to rise, while blue can cause your heart rate and blood pressure to decrease. In a West German study conducted in 1948, it was found that yellow, orange or red increased student IQ.

Color plays a critical role in our lives. In the chapter on fashion we'll discuss how certain colors look better on us and why.

## People and Things You are Grateful For:

1). _____
2). _____
3). _____
4). _____
5). _____
6). _____
7). _____
8). _____
9). _____
10). _____
11). _____
12). _____
13). _____
14). _____
15). _____
16). _____
17). _____
18). _____
19). _____
20). _____

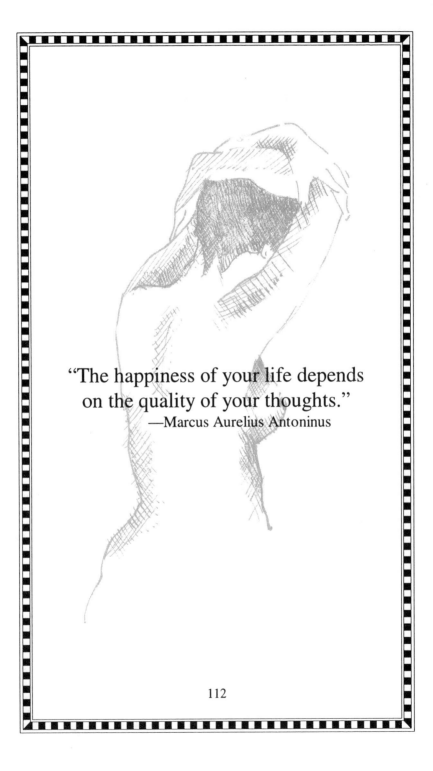

"The happiness of your life depends
on the quality of your thoughts."
—Marcus Aurelius Antoninus

# *Perception is Everything*

In order to change our lives, we must be willing to take total responsibility for ourselves and our experiences. We must stop viewing ourselves as victims and realize that in our positive, healthy new life there is no blame—there is only responsibility. There are no victims, only CO-creators. You may be saying to yourself, "What is she talking about? Of *course* there are victims." Trust me on this. You will come to realize that there are no victims.

There is nothing empowering about being a victim. The very label makes one feel helpless and give up. When we perceive ourselves as victims, we feel we're always at the mercy of someone or something else. As a CO-creator, however, we decide our own destiny. *We* are in control.

Remember, you can never effect a change outside yourself, without first effecting a change within.

All dissatisfaction with your life can be attributed to the difference between what is true and what you think is true. How you see your life cannot be any more or less than what you *believe* about your life, or what you believe you should see in your life. As I earlier quoted Dr. Maxwell Maltz as saying in his famous book *Psycho-Cybernetics*, "You act, and feel, not according to what things are really like, but according to the image your mind holds of what they are like."

Who you are and what you believe to be true is something *you* created. Your perception of life is a reflection of your beliefs. Your perception is quite literally your belief system, projected out into the world. Your perception is your viewpoint. Yours and yours alone.

Put your hands up against your eyes as if they were blinders (like the blinders on a horse). Now describe only what you see in your line of vision. Keeping your "blinders" on, make a ninety degree turn and describe what is now in your line of vision. You should be describing an entirely different picture.

Both pictures are accurate and limited in their perception. Take another ninety degree turn and you have another reality and another perception. Take another ninety degree turn, and then come full circle. You have now experienced the whole.

Each of us believes his or her view of the world is correct and accurate; but each of us is working with a limited picture, a picture colored by our own beliefs and perceptions. Hence the saying that we should not pass judgment on another until we have walked in their shoes.

Everything that seems to happen in the outside world is a direct reflection of what is going on in the subconscious part of your mind. The subconscious is where you hold your beliefs, your values. The subconscious bears total responsibility for your life experiences.

The human mind is the greatest computer that has ever been created. But as with all computers, "garbage in, garbage out". Imagine the conscious mind is like a window on the changing world (call it the floppy drive). It becomes aware of new things and compares them to the existing data in the subconscious mind (the hard drive), so it can decide what to retain and what to reject. Negative programming will keep you seeing and experiencing negative things.

It is discrepancies in the mind between truth and perceived truth which cause dissatisfaction; and it is inside the mind, not outside, where corrections must first be made. But how do we make the corrections? Perhaps an even more critical question is, how do we know what corrections to make

"If you can imagine it, you can achieve it; If you can dream it you can become it."

—Anonymous

# Mirror, Mirror, On the Wall...

Everything you observe mirrors what exists in your belief system. Everything you observe. For the next thirty days I want you to imagine that every person you come in contact with is your very own personalized healer. They are here on the planet with just one mission, and that mission is to help you become the most balanced, joy-filled, loving individual you can be.

Each of us possesses within us every possible quality and attribute, good and bad. We each possess love, hate, nobility, brutality, energy, laziness, joy, sorrow, compassion, contempt, pleasantness, pettiness—it's all in there. Every quality imaginable is within each and every one of us.

Everything we need in order to heal ourselves, we will see in, and pull from, one another. This is why someone may see good in a person when another sees bad.

We are capable of seeing only two kinds of things in other people— the things we need to forgive, and the things we need to be grateful for.

Let's imagine you have an encounter with a person, and they trigger mental images in you

117

which you then project back out onto them.

When you are experiencing warm, comfortable feelings, it's because the person is mirroring something you like about yourself, or something that you need to be grateful for. When an encounter triggers feelings of anger, guilt, frustration, disappointment, or annoyance, the person is reflecting something you do *not* like about yourself, or something that needs forgiveness.

Reverend Joan Gattuso in her book *A Course in Love* provides a wonderful exercise I would like you to try right now. Take a clean sheet of paper and draw a horizontal line across the top. From the center of that line draw a vertical line all the way down the page. Write the name of a person, who really pushes your buttons, at the top of the page. Then place a plus sign (+) on the left and a minus sign (-) on the right. Write down everything you like and admire about the person in the plus column. When you have absolutely exhausted the positives, move to the minus side and write down everything you *don't* like about the person.

One of my clients used her mother as an example. She said she and her mother couldn't be in the same room for more than 15 minutes before the mother had pushed every single one of her buttons. Her list looked like this:

Client's mother:

| + | - |
| --- | --- |
| Beautiful hair | Critical |
| Nice dresser | Judgmental |
| Good gardener | Nags |
| Very sociable | Complaining |
| Smart | Manipulating |
| Independent | Irrational |

The list is like a mirror being held up to your face. The qualities that you listed about the other person, both good and bad, are really about you. Before every item in the plus column add the words:

"I love myself when I am..."

Then go to the minus column and add the words:

"I *don't* love myself when I am..."

Mind you, this exercise can be brutal. My client recognized everything with the exception of the gardening. She said she didn't understand this one because she didn't garden. I asked her to look beneath the surface and tell me what the gardening represented to her. She said it represented being creative. Once she realized this, she agreed that it did fit after all. Usually the mirror will be obvious, but occasionally you have to search a bit.

I went through a period several years ago during which everyone I met was so judgmental that I couldn't believe it. Those who knew me would have told you I wasn't judgmental at all, so I couldn't figure out why I was perceiving judgment everywhere around me. Then my sister said to me, "You've become so self-critical and self-judging lately." Bingo—there it was. I saw it, forgave it and literally did not need to see it again. The next day all was back to normal.

I have a dear friend who married twice. Both husbands were emotionally abusive. She didn't get the mirror because she was not an abusive person—or so she thought. It wasn't until she was willing to take a look at her own *self*-abuse that she understood the mirror and was able to heal it.

Back to my client's list. After she added the words I suggested, it read as follows:

"I love myself when I have beautiful hair."
"I love myself when I dress nicely."
"I love myself when I am creative."
"I love myself when I am sociable."
"I love myself when I am smart."
"I love myself when I am independent."
"I don't love myself when I am critical."
"I don't love myself when I judge others."
"I don't love myself when I nag."

"I don't love myself when I'm complaining."
"I don't love myself when I'm manipulating."
"I don't love myself when I'm irrational."

You must understand that any attempt to change the other person, in hopes of relieving the discomfort, will be both frustrating and ineffective. The other person will view it as manipulation, and will resist, even fight any such attempt. To heal yourself you must *always* take responsibility and ask yourself, "What can this person teach me about myself? What can I learn from this person, and how can I heal myself?" Never place blame or judgment on others. It is at best unproductive, and in most cases is counter-productive and self-destructive.

Again, for the next thirty days imagine that everyone you come in contact with is your own personal healer. They love you very much, and want you to be healed so that you can live an unconditionally loving life. Look at each person with this new perspective, and see what you can learn about yourself. You'll be surprised, you'll learn a lot, and you'll put yourself on the road to healthy self-love.

Forgiveness is the only thing that can heal a sick relationship, especially your relationship with yourself. Forgiveness lets you heal yourself, and look at life from a brand new perspective, a perspective of responsibility rather than blame.

"Life is an exercise in forgiveness."
—Norman Cousins

# *Forgive, Forgive...*

Forgiveness is perhaps the hardest lesson to learn, yet the most healing one to master. When we refuse to forgive ourselves or someone else for something (whether as small as not phoning, or as horrific as killing someone), we literally hold that lack of forgiveness within our own spirit and body and make ourselves ill.

It may be hard to believe, but forgiveness is *not* something we do primarily for the *other* person. Forgiveness is something we must learn to do for *ourselves*. When I'm giving a talk, I often have people come up to me and ask how they can forgive someone who broke up their happy home, or someone who brutally murdered a family member, or even someone as monstrous as Hitler. My reaction is always the same. The other person is not really affected by your lack of forgiveness, but *you* are.

I don't mean in any way to make light of something as awful as a violent murder, or the brutal massacre of millions in the holocaust. But let's face it— the murderer is probably in jail and doesn't feel your hatred. Hitler is dead and definitely doesn't feel your hatred. Even a supposed friend who has caused you grief in some way probably doesn't have a clue about how you're really feeling. So who suffers with all this lack of forgiveness? You do.

When we refuse to forgive, we literally weaken ourselves. Through using applied kineseology (or what is sometimes called "muscle testing"), we can ask the body questions and get an amazingly accurate response. I could ask you to hold two brown paper bags, without knowing what was in either, and your body would tell me, through testing your muscle strength, if what was in each bag was good or bad for your body. One bag, for example, could be filled with grapes, and the other with processed sugar. You would not consciously know the contents—you might not even know which item was good for you and which wasn't—but your body would know the answers before you opened the bags and this knowing would be reflected in the strength or weakness of your muscles.

In the same sense, when we refuse to forgive, we hold the anger, hurt, and frustration within our own muscles and literally weaken them. If I were to ask you to think of someone you loved, and to hold the thought of that person in your mind's eye, and while you were thinking about that person I muscle tested you, I would find that your muscles remained strong. If, on the other hand, I asked you to hold the picture in your mind's eye of someone who had done you wrong or someone that you greatly disliked, and while you were holding this picture I muscle tested you, your muscles would literally weaken.

This clearly demonstrates how important forgiveness is to our overall health. Yet we always think that forgiveness is something we do for others. No, we should do it primarily for ourselves.

Speaking of ourselves, the most important person in the world to forgive is you. You *need* to forgive yourself first. What kinds of things do you need to forgive yourself for? You need to forgive yourself for not loving yourself exactly as you are, for not seeing your true potential, and for not living life with happiness and joy within your heart.

You need to forgive yourself for putting your life on hold until you lose weight, you get married, you find a new job, the kids are grown, etc. You need to realize that each day is unique, has never been here before and will never be here again. You need to live in the present, and be grateful for everything you experience during the course of the day. You need to be grateful for the spring rain, the smell of autumn leaves, the blue sky, water, clean air, a roof over your head, the people you love and who love you, the ordinary little joys that we overlook in our mad haste to get somewhere else. You need to forgive yourself for not seeing these small miracles, and for not acknowledging them.

But most of all you need to forgive yourself for not realizing what a miracle *you are*. There's no one like you in the whole world—in the entire Universe. You've so much to offer, to yourself and others, and yet you're wasting so much of your precious energy trying to reach for things that aren't even important.

You need to stop measuring your successes in life against someone else's yardstick, and measure them against your own. You alone know what you're capable of doing and how it needs to be done. Your special brand of love, kindness, generosity, joy, and happiness is unique. No one can bring that to the world but you.

Take the time to forgive yourself for the time you've wasted by not loving you for who you are, and really begin to enjoy your life and do great things for yourself and the world. I certainly forgive you for not seeing your greatness. Now, *you* just have to forgive *yourself.*

# Qualities You Like in Yourself:

1). _____
2). _____
3). _____
4). _____
5). _____
6). _____
7). _____
8). _____
9). _____
10). _____
11). _____
12). _____
13). _____
14). _____
15). _____
16). _____
17). _____
18). _____
19). _____
20). _____

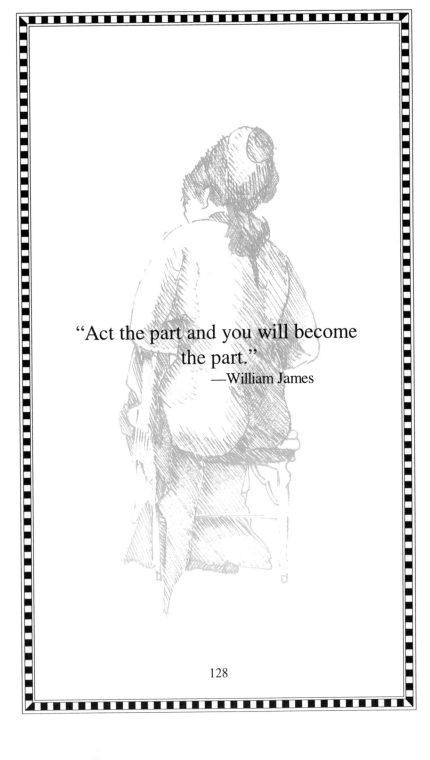

"Act the part and you will become the part."
—William James

# Eliminate the Negatives

I'm not going to lie to you. Most plus size people, especially plus size women, experience significant cultural bias. *Smithsonian Magazine* conducted a psychological study of 6-year-olds. They asked the children to take a look at the silhouettes of people of various sizes and shapes, and to describe what they thought the people would be like. When the children saw the silhouettes of fat people, they said that these people would be "ugly", "dirty", "stupid" and "lazy".

In 1995 John Stossel, on the ABC television magazine show *20/20*, asked first graders a series of questions to see if they had already been affected by any kind of cultural bias with regard to weight. He asked the children if they would rather be friends with an ugly person or a fat person, and the children screamed "ugly". He asked the children if they would rather be friends with a stupid person or a fat person, and the children screamed in unison "stupid". And then he asked the question which brought an astonishing, and heart-breaking, answer, "Would you rather have one arm or be fat?" They screamed "one arm."

On second thought, is this really all that surprising? Remember all the lovely little refrains from our own childhood, like "Fat, Fat, the water rat...", or "Fatty, fatty, two-by-four...?" Have things really changed all that much?

There's no question that the cultural bias against plus size people is significant; but when we tie our self-worth to our body size and/or shape, we are incredibly dis-empowered. Self-esteem should be tied to accomplishments, not body size, shape, or weight. So, why is our self-worth tied to the shape of our bodies? How did we begin to feel this way?

It happens first through what is called the "collective unconscious" (beliefs generated over time by many), as seen in the 6-year-old studies. And it happens second through the media—advertisements, television shows, movies, etc. The media have created the false image of the ideal woman—size 4-6, age 25, and 5' 10" tall.

You and I both know that this is not a real person. The fact is that only 1% of the population is genetically predisposed to being a size 4-6. Yet the other 99% of us strive to be this impossible dream, then beat ourselves up for not being able to achieve what is in almost all cases impossible to achieve. In other words, we believe we "failed", and this mentality promotes low self-esteem.

Eleanor Roosevelt said it perhaps better than anyone else ever has: "No one can make you feel inferior without your consent." This is absolutely true. So quit giving your consent.

We have over 50,000 thoughts a day. 80% of these thoughts are negative, and 90% of these thoughts are repeated daily—thoughts like, "I'm so fat. I'm ugly. This dress looks terrible on me. I've gained so much weight. I'm having a bad hair day", and on and on and on. The self-criticism is constant, and unrelenting.

Think about this—do you say nice things about yourself when you see yourself in a mirror or catch your reflection in a pane of glass? Do you see your image and begin the negative chatter, or do you stop, look yourself up and down and say, "Lookin' good!" You have so many positive characteristics, but you won't see them until you teach yourself to focus on those positives, instead of the negatives. We have to quit focusing on the flaws.

But before you start beating yourself up, you need to know that it is *not* your fault that you focus on the flaws. You were trained well. Beginning when we were babies, the word "no" became our mantra. The constant "no, don't touch that, don't do that, don't say that..." was enough to make you go mad. There was so much focus on what we *shouldn't* do, and so little on what we should.

Then we went off to school. When we took a test we would get it back graded with marks like "-10, -40 etc." instead of +90, +60. Once again, this just served to reinforce the negatives. How many of you received weekly allowances? Did you have them taken away if you did something wrong rather

131

than being rewarded with even more allowance for doing something right?

At the University of Iowa they conducted a study to find out just how many negatives we actually hear as a child. They assigned graduate students to mothers with two-year-old children, and spent the day with them in the mall. Each graduate student had two hand clickers. They were to record on the left clicker the number of times the children heard the mother make a negative statement, and use the right clicker to record the mother's positive statements to the child. At the end of the day, all the grad students brought in their clickers and the results were tallied. On average, a two-year-old heard 432 negatives and 32 positives.

Even our penal system is based upon negatives. Once again, we make much more use of the stick than the carrot. Instead of rewarding people for good behavior, we punish them for bad. This is based on the supposition that people are intrinsically good, and we certainly shouldn't be rewarding them for what they are inherently disposed to do. The problem with this theory is that we are social creatures. We need attention. And even attention for misbehavior is better than no attention at all. You can easily see that we have a lot of prisons filled with people who agree.

Let's go back to the "ideal woman", as seen by the media, and see just how foolish we are for trying to achieve this unattainable image. As I noted, she is size 4-6, yet we know that only about 1% of the population are genetically predisposed to being this size. We said that she is 5'10", yet the average height in America is 5'4". Perhaps the one that irks me the most is that she is 25 years old.

Between 1946 and 1964 over 76 million people were born. We call them the "baby boomers". Do the math. The *youngest* baby boomer is 34. This means that 76 million + people can never be 25 again. We are just as responsible for this fallacy as the media is, however, because we continue to buy into it.

By the industry's definition of plus size (size 12 and up), we plus size women represent a staggering 40% of the entire US population. In fact, more than a third of the female population over the age of 18 wear size 14 and above. The average dress size in America is 14, the average height is 5'4", the average age is 43, and as many women wear size 18 as wear size 8. It shouldn't surprise you to learn that the first clothes to sell out on QVC and The Home Shopping Network are plus size clothes.

Do these statistics in any way correlate with the way the media represents us? I don't think so. Go to the newsstand and get any bridal magazine. In many cases, 14-year-old girls are being photographed as the brides. 25-year-olds are being photographed as the *mothers* of the brides. *These* are our ideals? Is it any wonder we have huge increases in plastic surgery in this country every year? But here's the truth—I don't care how talented your plastic surgeon is, he isn't going to make you 25 again. Believe me when I tell you, today bodies are created at least as much by culture as they are by biology.

Things have gotten completely out of control when 94% of all women are dissatisfied with their bodies, 45% of underweight women feel as though they are too fat, and 28% of all college women suffer from bulimia (and this statistic is rising with incredible speed). Dieting has become the accepted norm, even though we know diets are 98% ineffective, and are in fact the fastest way to gain weight.

Your weight, your body shape, your size are not the issue. Self-esteem is always the issue! We need to begin to focus on the positives. The positives are right there within each and every one of us, but we just need to train ourselves to see them. Remember, what you focus on expands. If you focus on the flaws you will see more flaws. If you focus on the positives you will see more positives. Make it a habit to accentuate the positive. The choice is yours.

# Qualities You Would Like to Cultivate in Yourself:

1). _____
2). _____
3). _____
4). _____
5). _____
6). _____
7). _____
8). _____
9). _____
10). _____
11). _____
12). _____
13). _____
14). _____
15). _____
16). _____
17). _____
18). _____
19). _____
20). _____

"Belief in a thing makes it happen."
—Frank Lloyd Wright

# Grooming

I'm sure you'd agree that we women are judged by a harsher standard than men. But as unfair as it may seem, it is partially our own doing. We used to like being up on that traditional pedestal, until it became more and more work to remain there. Balancing on that pedestal is far too difficult now that we have everyday life to contend with.

But when we step down off the pedestal everyone is horrified, and gives us grief for not striking a more gorgeous, statuesque pose. This is a dilemma. What do we do? Well, we stop giving *ourselves* grief for not wanting to be on the pedestal anymore. Say, "I made a mistake, I don't like it up here, I'm tired and I want to eat", and step down.

It's true that we all like to be around beautiful people. Hundreds of studies have been conducted on what constitutes "beauty", and in every case weight, body shape, and size are never in the top three. The number one attribute of beauty is always—can you guess it? Grooming. That's right—grooming, followed closely by self-esteem and personality. These are the top three. Grooming defines beauty. Grooming is literally your self-esteem made visible.

Have you ever been working out in the yard, and suddenly decided to go into town, or to the mall, to get something? You figure you don't have to get cleaned up, because "Who's gonna see me?" Right? Wrong! You get there and it's as if the Wicked Witch of the West had spelled your name in the sky, and told the world to hurry, because they won't believe what they're about to see. You run into people you haven't seen in 10 years. And they want to introduce you to the new neighbors. Or worse yet, they introduce you to their husband's best friend, who's attractive, intelligent, witty and single.

You try to laugh it off and make feeble excuses (anything, even the truth, is a feeble excuse) as to why you look so dreadful. They say, "Oh, don't be silly, you look fine. After all, who looks good after working in the yard anyway?" Of course, when they get out of hearing range they say, "I can't *believe* how bad Debbie looked. She's *really* let herself go."

Now you may think this isn't important, but it is. First, if you haven't seen these people in 10 years, they may not really know that you clean up quite nicely, thank you very much, and so they're telling *everyone* what a wreck you are. Thoughts are energy; and believe me this isn't the best energy to have floating around.

Even more important, however, is the fact that you didn't put your best foot forward. You didn't look your best, so you didn't feel your best; and by not feeling your best, you went automatically back to being hard on yourself, with the consequence that you wind up feeling even *worse* about yourself. We can't afford too many of those moments, can we?

Finally, you may have just become someone's negative belief system. We learn from modeling, not information. Let's go back to the *Smithsonian Magazine* study of six-year-olds and the fat silhouettes from the previous chapter. Just reading that study has no major impact on the person reading it, *unless* they have a model by which they can verify the validity of the "information"—in this case, fat people are ugly, dirty, stupid and lazy.

But let's say the next day on the way to work, someone who read about that study sees a plus size woman with dirty, wrinkled clothes, filthy hair, no makeup, and bad posture getting out of her car with a jelly doughnut in her mouth. The jelly drips down the front of her soiled blouse as she shuffles along. Now, suddenly, the person has a model for the information he or she read the night before. Now it's a belief, a demonstrated absolute. With all the negative body messages we already have, we certainly can't afford to become someone else's negative role model.

Information + Verification = Belief

55% of the first impression you make is based on your appearance and your actions. What's really amazing is that it takes only about 7 seconds to create an image impact. That means that in the first

7 seconds after meeting you, perhaps before you even open your mouth, someone is making conscious and unconscious judgments about you based on your appearance alone.

They're judging your economic level, your educational level, your social position, your level of sophistication, degree of success, moral character, trustworthiness, and more—all in just 7 seconds. Frightening, isn't it? And remember, you never get a second chance to make that first impression.

Your posture makes one of the most important statements about you in that first 7 seconds. Posture is an instant indicator of high or low self-esteem. Good posture not only indicates the person has self-respect, but it also shows that they are "comfortable in their space".

Good posture is very empowering. Try it. Sit in a chair. Roll your shoulders forward, let your head and neck fall down. Feel how lacking in energy, how hopeless you feel. Now, roll your shoulders back, lift your head and neck, and imagine that there's a string that goes from your chest through the bottom of your chin out the top of your head to the ceiling, and is being pulled taught. How does this feel? After getting over the initial awkwardness of it, it should feel incredibly empowering. Practice good posture daily. It's not only good for your spine, but it's also good for your image.

As John Wesley wrote, "Cleanliness is, indeed, next to Godliness." Make sure you and your clothes are clean at all times. No one should have to be offended by being with you. Your hair, breath, body, finger and toenails should all be clean and well cared for.

Have you ever been sick in bed for several days? You lie there, feeling awful, until you're persuaded to get up and take a bath or shower. As soon as you do, you can't believe how much better you feel. This is so basic and so true. Personal cleanliness should be a way of living for you.

Make sure you keep your home clean as well. Dirt really does keep the energy of life from flowing through us.

In May of this year, I called in a wonderful feng shui practitioner by the name of Elaine Bartlett, from Boca Raton, Florida, to feng shui my house. I knew nothing about feng shui, and was surprised when she gave me a list of things she wanted me to clean. I was very skeptical as I was cleaning, but I also wanted to try this fashionable new "in thing" for myself. I must tell you, I just couldn't believe it. My life turned around immediately.

When I removed the clutter from my home, I simultaneously removed it from my life. This, coupled with some feng shui cures she provided, was the boost I needed to get the energy flowing in my life once again.

Being clean and well groomed has so many advantages. First, when you look your best, you feel good; and when you feel good, you put your best foot forward. Second, if you're well groomed you won't be promoting negative stereotypes about plus size women—you'll be doing your part to counteract that negativity. Be part of the solution, not the problem.

# What Could You Do Today To Become a Better Person:

1). _____
2). _____
3). _____
4). _____
5). _____
6). _____
7). _____
8). _____
9). _____
10). _____
11). _____
12). _____
13). _____
14). _____
15). _____
16). _____
17). _____
18). _____
19). _____
20). _____

"Real confidence comes from knowing and accepting yourself— your strengths and your limitations—in contrast to depending on affirmation from others, from outside."
—Judith M. Bardwick

# Thoughts are Energies

Shakespeare said it best when he said, "There is nothing either good or bad but thinking makes it so." It really is true that your thinking creates your reality. Your thoughts are perhaps even more powerful than your actions.

Have you ever run into someone you don't particularly care for? (And you know they don't like you any more than you like them.) You say, "Hi, how are you?" and they say, "It's so good to see you, I'm fine thank you, and how about you?" On the surface it sounds like you're long-lost pals, but you could cut the tension in the air with a butter knife.

Why? Because while you're saying one thing, your thoughts are saying, "Oh good grief, it's you. I can't believe it—I have one day off and I have to run into you." While the other person's thinking, "I can't stand you. The very sight of you has ruined my day." Believe me, it's your thoughts that are transmitted, not your words.

The truth of the matter is no one can ruin your day unless you allow them to. In fact, no one can hurt your feelings. It's not what I say to you that matters. It's what you say to *yourself* after I stop talking that counts. For example, what would you think if I said, "You have such purple hair?" You'd think I was having a bad day, because you know that you don't have purple hair.

But what if I said, "You're so fat and ugly?" Well, if you *believe* that you're fat and ugly, you're going to act hurt by my words. But in fact it is not my words that have hurt you, but rather your own self-doubt. Your own self-doubt was already present before I said the words. I just brought your self-doubt to the surface. You literally weaken your body, hurt yourself, and limit yourself with your own self-doubt.

A study conducted at Tufts University found through using kineseology that your muscles became weak when you doubt yourself. Just by saying the word "can't" you will literally weaken yourself. It was further found that lying disoriented the brain. If you were to repeat the phrase "I'm a bad girl" over and over your muscles would go weak. If you were to repeat "I'm a good girl" over and over your muscles would remain strong.

This is because you're not a bad girl. You're lying to yourself and disorienting your brain when you tell yourself negative things about yourself. This negativity is literally lying to the brain. When you find yourself saying the word "can't" stop yourself immediately and say "Cancel", then affirm that you *can* do something.

Incidentally, when you're affirming you want to make your affirmations in the present tense, and

you want to preface them with the words "I'm...".
If you remove something from your subconscious,
like a negative belief, you have to replace it with a
positive immediately. Removing anything creates a
vacuum, and unless you immediately fill it with a
positive, you will gradually refill that space with
more of what you had before—negative thoughts.

You have no control over what other people
say and do to you—none whatsoever. But you *do*
have 100% control over *how you feel and respond*
to what they say or do.

Jack Canfield has a wonderful equation that I
urge you to remember:

Events + Response = Outcome

You can't change the event because you have
no control over it. But you can change the outcome
by changing the only thing you do have control
over—your response.

Imagine this scenario: You're about to pull out
into a street. It looks as though the coast is clear,
but as soon as you pull out someone comes very
fast over the hill. He honks his horn and flashes you
the finger and you respond in kind, flashing him the
finger back and muttering obscenities. You get angry, and you're so upset and distracted that you go
through a red light and get a ticket. Your day is ruined.

Now picture the scenario just a little differently. You still pull out in front of the car and the

person still flashes you the finger, but instead of simply returning the same negative energy, you smile at him, shrug your shoulders and say, "I'm sorry". You can literally see the anger dissipate on the other person's face. You're fine, you don't go through the red light, or get a ticket, or ruin your day. Same event, different response, different outcome.

We have to learn that what we're thinking, both consciously and unconsciously at any moment, creates our realities. Our beliefs are constantly searching for outside data to verify them. In order to create a happier, healthier, more loving and successful life, we have to remove the limiting, negative beliefs. How do we do that? Well, first we need to know how beliefs are created in the first place.

Beliefs are created in three ways. First they're created in what are called the "pre-critical years", from birth to age 8. We have no way of knowing if things are true or false, so we take the word of someone in authority for our beliefs.

Did you grow up hearing that if you went outside with wet hair you would catch a cold? If you did, I'm sure you found it to be true. Yet, if you didn't grow up hearing this and don't have it in your belief system, I'm sure you've never gotten a cold by going outside with your hair wet. Neither belief is right or wrong. It's just a belief.

Second, we create beliefs in moments of intense emotion—something that is usually a negative event, like having a fight with someone we love. I have a friend who is gorgeous, but one day in the middle of a nasty fight, her soon-to-be ex-husband told her she looked like a gargoyle without her makeup on. She was so upset that from that day forward she wouldn't leave her room before she had full makeup on. She wouldn't even let her children see her without makeup.

Last, we create beliefs while we're asleep, in shock, or under anesthesia. This is good news, because it is while we're asleep that we can go into the subconscious and remove the negative limiting beliefs and replace them with positive ones. Knowing that we create beliefs while we're asleep, however, should stop you from falling asleep to television or radio ever again.

The brain has four brain wave cycles. Beta is the cycle we're in when we're awake and working, talking, playing, etc. Alpha is the next level down, and is the state where we're physiologically relaxed and psychologically alert. As I mentioned earlier, this is where most great artists of all kinds create their work. The next level down is Theta, and finally Delta. It is in theta that we can re-program the subconscious. But how to do that?

Here at Blueberry Hill we use the work of Dr. Teri Mahaney, who wrote the book and tape series *Change Your Mind*. Teri put Dr. Georgi Lozanov's work in music and sound together with the work of Dr. Lloyd Silverman.

Dr. Silverman was working with the effects of

subliminals on schizophrenics, and found that a simple five word sentence, when delivered subliminally to his patients, had a remarkably healing effect. That sentence was, "Mommy and I are one." Through combining the work of these two researchers she created *Change Your Mind*.

She created, recorded, and listened to a script on being more organized, and nothing seemed to be happening until one day she fell asleep while listening to the script. Within the next few days she noticed that her desk was clean and the paperwork was done. She says her contribution was that she fell asleep. And what a glorious sleep it was for all of us.

In this program you create and record a script in your own voice that you listen to for 10-30 nights (depending on the script) while you're sleeping. You remove the negative beliefs and replace them with positive ones at the subconscious level. Your life can be totally transformed in 30 days.

At Blueberry Hill we work with people at the subconscious level to clear negative beliefs by using Dr. Mahaney's work. We also teach her program as a stand-alone seminar throughout the year. You can begin to increase your self-esteem and rid yourself of negative beliefs immediately.

Years ago, when I was taking acting lessons, I learned two approaches to acting. The first was called "method acting", originally developed and taught by the famous Russian actor Stanislavsky and later refined and taught by Lee Strasberg and

Elia Kazan at the Actors Studio in New York. Prime examples of method actors would be Marlon Brando, James Dean, Paul Newman, Al Pacino, and Dustin Hoffman. The second was called "technique acting", and perhaps the best example of this would be the great British actor Sir Laurence Olivier.

In method acting you created your character from the inside out, by doing a psychological study, figuring out their emotions, intentions, etc. In technique acting you created the character from the outside in, starting with the physical characteristics. You dressed like the character, walked like the character, talked like the character and pretty soon got inside and became the character. Neither was better or worse—they were just different ways of achieving the same goals.

The same holds true for increasing self-esteem. You can work from the inside out by re-programming the subconscious mind, using programs such as Dr. Mahaney's; or you can do the 21-Day assignment in the back of the book and "fake it till you make it", so to speak. (Remember, your subconscious doesn't know the difference.)

At Blueberry Hill we use everything we can to help you "eliminate the negatives" and re-program with the positives. Instead of spending time trying to become an impossible image, we teach you how to become the best you that you can possibly be. We teach you to love the person you already are—right here, right now. If you're seeking an authentic woman, a remarkable woman, a gorgeous woman, you don't have to look any farther than your own mirror. You're a masterpiece!

# People or Organizations You Need to Forgive:

1). _____
2). _____
3). _____
4). _____
5). _____
6). _____
7). _____
8). _____
9). _____
10). _____
11). _____
12). _____
13). _____
14). _____
15). _____
16). _____
17). _____
18). _____
19). _____
20). _____

"How many cares one loses when one decides not to be something, but to be someone."
—Coco Gabrielle Chanel

# Fashion Friendly Facts

When it comes to fashion, there's more and more for us to choose from. Designers and manufacturers are realizing that plus size women have disposable incomes and are ready and willing to spend their dollars on clothes that make them feel and look their best. When you are looking for fashion, there are some things in particular you should be looking for.

First, get your colors analyzed by a licensed image consultant. I see so many women who would look great if only they were wearing the right colors. The best looking outfit on the hanger can make you look sickly if it isn't the right color for *you*. You want your clothes to enhance who you are. You don't want them to be so loud they leave you behind, and you don't want them to wash you out. Make color your number one priority.

Different body types look better in certain styles of clothes. The key to dressing correctly for your body type, however, is balance. You want to make sure that you have balanced the body. An important thing to remember is that you are only as wide as your widest line, so you want to find the widest line on your body and then make the visual corrections to the body in order to make the body appear as though it is in balance.

Fashion comes and goes, but "Style" is eternal! All the top designers agree that it's style that makes the woman. But how do you create your own personal style on a limited budget? Accessories!

Accessorizing is an easy, inexpensive way to create many different looks. A few accessory changes here and there can change the look of an outfit, and double or triple its usefulness. Accessories are a vital part of every wardrobe. They're fun, creative, and reflect your personality, without necessarily spending a fortune. Accessories can focus attention where you want it and redirect the eye away from trouble spots.

Proportion is one of the key elements in choosing the right accessories. We full-figured women should wear accessories that are scaled up in size, but not so much that the accessory is all anyone notices. Accessories need to be balanced— no one accessory should be so big or bold as to detract from your total look. "Keep it Simple".

Don't wear an accessory so small that you can't see it. When something is too small for you it makes you look bigger—this goes for clothing as well. Don't pay any attention to the size on the label. Pay attention to how it looks on your body. When it fits well, you'll look better. Back to accessories.

Jewelry, more than any other accessory, expresses your personality. There's no better way to conceal figure flaws. Jewelry can draw attention to or from body areas and dress an outfit up or down. It doesn't need to be real, but it does need to have impact. Those small genuine pieces may possess sentimental value but they won't create the impact a well-designed and well-chosen piece of good costume jewelry can.

Earrings are the most important accessory you can buy. When buying earrings consider the shape of your face, the size of your earlobe, and the length of your neck.

A pin can bring the focus to the face without cutting the body. It adds pizzazz without a lot of hassle, and should be worn high on the shoulder. Necklaces can be great if you choose the right length. For understated elegance, pearls are a must! If you have a double chin, or a short neck, stay away from a choker; and if you're well endowed, choose necklaces that stop above the cleavage. Choose rings as an accessory if your nails are well groomed. And while were on the subject of nails— even they can become an accessory if painted.

Scarves are a great way to brighten up or tone down an outfit. A colorful scarf, at the neckline, can make that not too flattering top you bought look great.

Shoes are the most accurate index of taste. The most elegant and costly of outfits can be instantly cheapened by badly chosen or poorly cared for shoes. Don't scrimp on your shoes. Straps across the instep or around the ankle make the leg look shorter and larger. A low heel is best with pants and a 1½"-2" heel is best with skirts. If you wear open toed shoes make sure your feet are well groomed.

When it comes to purses, think quality over quantity. Make certain you choose a handbag that suits your needs, and your size. A purse that's too small makes a woman look bigger. Pay close attention to where the bag hits you—that's where you'll direct the viewer's focus. Your purse and shoes don't have to match, but they should blend.

In general, a belt looks best on a body that has a defined waistline. Since belts create a strong horizontal line across the body I suggest that you wear a belt that's the same color as the outfit you're wearing.

Hats give a person presence and stand out as a signature piece. The key to wearing a hat is to wear it with confidence. The shape of your hat should compliment the shape of your body and face. The taller you are the wider the brim can be, but never wider than your shoulders. Always look in a full length mirror to judge the proportion of the hat to your body size. Hats command attention, so as someone once aptly stated, "If you're not in the mood for comments, you're not in the mood for a hat."

Gloves are a necessary item if you live in a cold climate. Coordinate your gloves with your winter coat.

The "conservative" rule when it comes to hosiery is to wear sheer pantyhose in a neutral tone that makes your legs look slightly tan. Black skirts look great with black hose, but avoid most color hose, since an incorrect color match is definitely not a good look. White and patterned hose tend to make the leg look larger. The dressier the shoe, the more sheer the hose; and the sportier the shoe, the more opaque the hose.

One of the biggest problems I have with plus size women is to get them to buy clothes that fit. Most of us wait to buy clothes until we have lost 20 pounds. We keep waiting and waiting and buy only those clothes that will get us by. Whether you lose that 20 pounds or not is not important.

What *is* important is that you look your best *now*—not some time in the future but now. When you look good, you feel good about yourself; and in the meantime, you may just find yourself getting your body where you want it to be naturally.

Make certain that you own at least one outfit you can pull from your closet at any time and know that you will look your best. I call this a power outfit. Every woman should have at least one no matter what the cost. If you really look, you'll be able to find terrific values.

Many women are fashionable, but few have style. Fashions come and go with the seasons, but how you wear your clothes reflects your personal style. Style is self confidence made visible. Our style doesn't just express us—it literally reveals us.

And the good news is that it can be learned. Fashion is in the clothes, but style is in the wearer. Fashion is constantly changing, but like the wearer, style evolves.

Take the time to look good and to create your own inimitable style. You'll look and feel your ultimate best.

# *People or Organizations that Need to Forgive You:*

1). _____
2). _____
3). _____
4). _____
5). _____
6). _____
7). _____
8). _____
9). _____
10). _____
11). _____
12). _____
13). _____
14). _____
15). _____
16). _____
17). _____
18). _____
19). _____
20). _____

"It is certain because it is possible."
—Tertullian

# Appendix A

## 21-Day Assignment

It takes 21 consecutive days to create a habit. If you miss a day, you have to start again. This assignment is divided into two lists—the "must do" list and the "should do" list. I promise you that if you commit to doing everything on the "must do" list for 21 consecutive days, you will begin to feel great about yourself. You're worth it! Make the commitment to yourself to live a happier life. Everyone will benefit from your decision. Everyone.

### Must Do List:

1).* First thing in AM, for 5 minutes stand naked in front of a full-length mirror—start at your head and work down to toes, telling each body part something nice.
2). Increase movement—walk.
3). Be well-groomed at all times.
4). Maintain good posture.
5).* Eliminate judgment of self and others.

6).* No talking about looks or diets with any one.

7).* "Cancel" your negative thoughts and replace with positive ones.

8).* Acknowledge your successes daily—use a journal.

9). Stop saying "Can't".

10). Bless all your food before eating.

11). Never eat or drink in your car—*never*!

12). Compliment a minimum of three people every day.

13).* 5 minutes before bed, look into your eyes in the mirror and say nice things to yourself about yourself

## Shoul∂ Do ℒist:

1). Set a goal and accomplish it.

2). Get a make-over.

3). Get a massage.

4). Get a manicure and/or pedicure.

5). Concentrate on healthier eating.
Eliminate junk food.

6). Clean your house and car.

7). Clean out your closet.

8). Buy a power outfit (an outfit you know you can count on to always look good in).

9). Sign up to do or learn something you've been wanting to do or learn.

10). Volunteer time to a cause dear to your heart.
11). When stressed, listen to the Largo movements of Baroque music and in hale the scent of lavender.
12). Work in the garden. If you don't have one, start one. If you can't start one, borrow one. Find a way—or make one.

* It's important that you say nice things to yourself in a mirror, since you want to break that old habit of saying unkind things. You want the mirror to become your friend.

* You need to eliminate all judgment of yourself and others. When we place a judgment on some-one, it says a whole lot more about us than it does about the other person. Face it, the only real reason anyone ever has for judging another is because they feel so poorly about themselves that they need to put someone else down in order to feel better about themselves. You're not going to feel negatively about yourself any longer, so there will be no more need for this kind of behavior.

* Don't talk with anyone about diets or looks. Make certain that you take the focus off your body. If someone starts this kind of conversation with you, let them know that you're on a 21-day program and you will not be discussing those topics for the next 21 days. Perhaps you will pique their interest and you may be able to get them to join you on the program.

* When you catch your mind chattering negative self messages, verbalize (so you can hear it with your ears) the word "Cancel". Then replace the negative message with a positive one. You must get used to correcting the negative chatter.

* It's important that you end your day feeling good about yourself. Studies show that information that you take in just before you go to bed is repeated by your subconscious an average of 16 times during the night, while information taken in during the course of the day will be repeated by your subconscious only an average of 4 times. You want to take advantage of all that extra processing by making sure you say positive things to yourself about yourself just before you go to bed. Remember, it takes 21 consecutive days to create a habit and sometimes you've got to fake it until you make it.

# Appendix B

## How to Contact Your Guardian Angels

Sit in a comfortable chair with your eyes closed and your feet firmly on the floor. Take a deep breath in through the nose, breathing in the thoughts of light, love, joy, and healing, then exhale the breath out through your mouth, exhaling thoughts of frustration, anger, fear, remorse. Repeat this 5-10 times until you feel a sense of calm and relaxation come over you.

When you feel relaxed say, "I want to know the name of the angel sitting on my left shoulder now." Don't place any judgments, but trust that the first name that comes into your mind is the correct name, even if you don't know of anyone with that name or know of the name itself. After you have this name, say, "I want to know the name of the angel sitting on my right shoulder now." Again, don't judge. Just take the name that pops into your mind. You now know the names of the angels that are currently with you and you can call them by name and ask for their help and guidance. They really are there and they really want to help you—trust in this.

# About the Author

**Deborah Lynn Darling** is a down-to-earth, funny, warm, women, both witty *and* wise—a woman who, like you, has been there and done that—has been through the weight loss and gain cycle many times, and who has learned the hard way, not just that diets don't work, but why they don't work. She'll teach you how to transform your life in 30 days just by following her simple, easy, effective 21 day program for increasing self-esteem.

Deborah is the owner and director of Blueberry Hill Retreat for plus size women in Garrettsville, Ohio. She is a motivational speaker who conducts powerful, provocative seminars on personal transformation and growth, from one coast to the other, and is a highly-sought-after private counselor. In addition, she is a plus size model, an on-camera and voice over personality for some of America's best known companies, and has appeared on numerous radio and television shows, including *The Oprah Winfrey Show*.

Darling is the Associate Editor for *The Shifting Times* news magazine and writes her own newspaper column entitled "Fitting In". She is a singer/songwriter and the author of *The Upsize Woman in a Downsize World* book and tape series and the author of *Blueberry Hill: The Power of Love,* a book for children.

# *Miscellaneous:*

Deborah Darling is available for:

> Conference presentations
> Workshops
> Business and corporate counseling
> Keynotes, lectures and seminars

She can be reached through:
> Radiance Seminars
> P.O. Box 98
> Garrettsville, Ohio 44231
> (330) 527-2407
> email: radianceseminars@juno.com

To order her book or tape series entitled *Upsize Woman in a Downsize World*™ contact Radiance Publishing at (330) 527-2407.

For information on Blueberry Hill Retreat call (330) 527-5068.

For information on how to order Nicole LaVoie's *Sound Wave Energy* tapes or her book *Return to Harmony* or how to order Dr. Teri Mahaney's *Change Your Mind* book and tape series contact Radiance Seminars at (330) 527-2407.

# Notes

# Notes

# Notes

# Notes

# Notes

# Notes

# Notes